teachers for the real world

B. OTHANEL SMITH in collaboration with SAUL ~~COHEN~~ and ~~ARTHUR~~ ~~for~~ the
TASK FORCE of the NDEA National ~~in Teaching Disadvan~~

THE AMERICAN ASSOCIATION OF COLLEGES FOR TEACHER EDUCATION

ii

The materials in this publication were developed by the NDEA National Institute for Advanced Study in Teaching Disadvantaged Youth pursuant to a contract with the U. S. Department of Health, Education, and Welfare, Office of Education (Contract Number OEC 3-6-002042-2042). The Project was administered by the American Association of Colleges for Teacher Education in conjunction with Ball State University, Muncie, Indiana. Contractors undertaking such projects under government sponsorship are encouraged to express their judgment in professional and technical matters. Points of view or opinions do not, therefore, necessarily represent official Office of Education position or policy.

Published by
The American Association of Colleges for Teacher Education
1201 Sixteenth Street, N.W., Washington, D. C. 20036

Standard Book Number: 910052-02-6
Library of Congress Catalog Card Number: 71-76465

MEMBERS OF NATIONAL STEERING COMMITTEE AND TASK FORCE

HOBERT W. BURNS — *Vice President for Academic Affairs, San Jose State College, California*

SAUL B. COHEN — *Dean, Graduate School, Clark University, Worcester, Massachusetts*

WILLIAM E. ENGBRETSON — *Professor of Higher Education, Temple University, Philadelphia, Pennsylvania*

RICHARD L. FOSTER — *Superintendent of Schools, San Ramon Valley Unified School District, Danville, California*

VERNON HAUBRICH — *Professor of Education, University of Wisconsin, Madison, Wisconsin*

WILLIAM C. KVARACEUS — *Chairman, Department of Education, Clark University, Worcester, Massachusetts*

ARTHUR PEARL — *Professor of Education, University of Oregon, Eugene, Oregon*

F. GEORGE SHIPMAN — *Chairman, Department of Education, North Carolina College at Durham, North Carolina*

B. OTHANEL SMITH — *Chairman, Department of History and Philosophy of Education, University of Illinois, Urbana, Illinois*

JAMES R. TANNER — *Assistant Superintendent of Schools, Cleveland Public Schools, Ohio*

MATTHEW J. TRIPPE — *Professor of Education, University of Michigan, Ann Arbor, Michigan*

FOREWORD

This book presents a call for change in teacher education. The dimensions and directions of these changes have been identified and developed during the past two years by the Steering Committee and Task Force of the National Institute for Advanced Study in Teaching Disadvantaged Youth. They are offered as a stimulant and a contribution to the growing dialogue on teacher education for the future and are not to be viewed as a definitive program to be adopted as presented. The Committee's experience in clarifying the current situation in teacher education has emphasized the need to keep the dialogue open for new ideas and real differences of opinion and belief in specifying ends and means for the future. It should be noted that the recommendations and proposals of TEACHERS FOR THE REAL WORLD reflect the general position of the members of the National Committee and do not necessarily represent the points of view of the U. S. Office of Education, the American Association of Colleges for Teacher Education, or Ball State University. The Committe has taken seriously its charge to act as "man thinking" and to speak and act for itself.

The NDEA National Institute for Advanced Study in Teaching Disadvantaged Youth was established in June 1966 under a Title XI contract betwen the U. S. Office of Education and Ball State University, Muncie, Indiana. Administration of the Institute was subcontracted by the university to the American Association of Colleges for Teacher Education. Policy development and program planning for the Institute were delegated by the AACTE Executive Committee to a twelve-man National Institute Steering Committee and Task Force whose members were selected by the Committee in consultation with representatives of the Division of Educational Personnel Training, Bureau of Elementary and Secondary Education, U. S. Office of Education. They were chosen to be broadly representative of university and school personnel who were competent specialists in the education of the disadvantaged and in the preparation of teachers for work with educationally deprived children and youth.

From its inception, the NDEA National Institute has had as one of its major purposes the development of a structure through which National Committee members and their invited consultants could clarify the problems and issues which confront teacher education and assess the long-range needs of teacher education. It was to recommend to the Office of Education, the AACTE, and the profession at large improved programs for the preparation of teachers (especially for work with the disadvantaged) and useful strategies for implementing the changes in teacher education which would make it more relevant to the demands of our times. The Committee's monthly Task Force seminars from July 1966 through May 1968 were designed to deal with this purpose of the Institute.

In addition, the National Institute was charged with the planning and support of projects which would have an immediate and positive impact on programs for the preparation of teachers for the disadvantaged. Such field activities were planned and developed to effect change in the local situation and to provide the National Committee with feedback regarding the issues and problems which were the substance of its considerations of long-range plans and recommendations.

In its role as Steering Committee, the National Committee developed policies for the operation of the Institute, constructed guidelines for the selection and encouragement of field projects, and supervised the broad range of conferences, demonstrations, studies, publications and related activities which constituted the Institute's program. Reports on each of the specific components of the Institute program have been prepared by the Institute staff and published by the AACTE.

Although the responsibility for developing and coordinating the action phases of the National Institute was demanding and time-consuming for the members of the National Committee and its staff, the Committee was able to devote increasing amounts of time in its monthly meetings over the two years of its existence to the requirements of its role as "Task Force." In one of their early meetings, the members of the Committee identified the issues which appeared to be crucial to the development of immediate, as well as long-range, changes in teacher education. Members of the Committee and invited consultants prepared and presented position papers on selected issues and problems. Out of the discussions which developed around these presentations and around the reports from and reactions to the Institute's field activities came a decision to prepare a prospectus on teacher education for the future. It was agreed that such a prospectus, or call for change, would provide a more valuable end-product of the Institute's operations than would the usual "final report" of such enterprises. As originally planned, the prospectus was to have been an edited compilation of papers prepared by members of the Committee and revised on the basis of their discussion within the Task Force. As is frequently true with a group of highly committed and heavily burdened men, this original plan was modified by the realities of time and writing talent availabilities. Fortunately for the Committee, one of its members, B. Othanel Smith, was willing and able to accept the demanding assignment of compiling the diverse views of Committee members into a comprehensive statement on teacher education for the future. Two additional members of the Committee, Saul B. Cohen and Arthur Pearl, were selected to serve as members of an Editorial Committee under Smith's chairmanship.

The broad outline for the contents of the Committee's final substantive publication was developed by Smith and revised several times on the basis of extended discussions within the total Committee. A number of Committee members developed specific working materials which he incorporated into the manuscript. Although Smith is truly the major author, if not *the* author, of this volume, his work reflects the agreements and disagreements that became clear during the Committee's extensive discussions and stands in general as the Committee's statement. Each member of the Committee has had an opportunity to review and influence the development of each of the chapters in the book. Cohen and Pearl, as members of the Editorial Committee with Smith, have given the manuscript special review and have met with him to revise the final product. Special assistance in this review process also was provided from outside the Committee by Harry Broudy, Professor of Education, and Rupert Evans, Dean, College of Education, at the University of Illinois; and by James Hall, Jr., Education Specialist, Office of Planning, Program Review, and Research, Peace Corps, Washington, D. C.; Paul Ward, Executive Secretary, American Historical Association, Washington, D. C.; Joseph Young, Executive Director, National Advisory Council on Education Professions Development; Anthony Milazzo, University of Michigan; Rev. Joseph P. Owens, S.J., John Carroll University; John Pole, Ball State University; and David D. Darland, National Commission on Teacher Education and Professional Standards. The comments and suggestions of these men have been especially helpful and are sincerely appreciated.

As Director of the NDEA National Institute for the period of its existence, I have been privileged and challenged in working with the highly competent and uniquely individual men who have served as members of the National Committee and as its regular consultants and liaison representatives from related organizations and agencies. On behalf of the Association, as well as for myself personally, it is a pleasure to thank them publicly for their contributions to the work of the Institute.

No printed word of thanks will do justice to the debt which the Committee, the staff, and the Association owe to B. O. Smith. His unbelievable industry and productivity, and his ability to subjugate his personal interests to the group's good make him a professional's professional. We are pleased to hear ourselves speaking through his cogent words.

Finally, a special word of appreciation to Donald N. Bigelow, who fathered the idea of the National Institute from his position of leadership in the Office of Education; to Edward C. Pomeroy, Executive Secretary of AACTE, who encouraged and enabled the Association to develop the notion of a National Institute; and to John R. Emens, who, as President of Ball State University, made it possible for the Institute to become a reality.

RICHARD E. LAWRENCE
Director

December, 1968

PREFACE

This book outlines a plan for the education of the nation's teachers. It is a product of the NDEA National Institute for Advanced Study in Teaching Disadvantaged Youth. In the course of its deliberations, the Institute Task Force came to consider teacher education more and more as a whole, to attribute failures and inadequacies of education for the disadvantaged to defects in the education of teachers. In consequence, the Task Force undertook to explore the issues in teacher education and to set forth the outlines of a plan of education to prepare teachers for all children, regardless of their cultural backgrounds or social orgins. This book is an outcome of that enterprise. While education of the disadvantaged is the touchstone of the plan, the focus of the essay is a comprehensive, basic program of teacher education.

The nation is in a period of profound discontent, erupting now and then into social convulsions. Some of this unrest springs from dissatisfaction with the total educational system. This is a time for both immediate action and long-range educational planning. It is a time for radical reforms in teacher education as well as in all other educational programs.

Teacher education is at a critical point in its history. There is now enough knowledge and experience to reform it, to plan a basic program of teacher education for an open society in a time of upheaval. But if this knowledge and experience are dissipated in prolonged discussions of issues, doctrines, and tenets leading only to *more* dialogue, instead of a fundamental program of education for the nation's teachers, teacher education is likely to fragment and its pieces drift in all directions. The likelihood of either of these alternatives has influenced this essay. The reader will find very little discussion of issues and doctrines. Instead, he will find the outlines of a plan of teacher education ranging from the teacher aide to the beginning teacher. The plan is based largely on what is known about training, about the uses of theory, about teaching, and about social realities.

No claim is made that the suggested plan is ideal. It is hoped that it will lead to a workable program, one more in line with the knowledge and social realities of our time than existing programs in and out of higher institutions. The path to a better program is not a marble stairway with its base resting upon unshakable knowledge. It is a treacherous path where the safety of no step is sure, and what little security exists is based upon the interplay of a number of elements, each independently supported and often incapable, individually, of bearing much weight. The task is first to formulate a basic program, building it step by step on what meager knowledge we have; then to strengthen it as further experience indicates defects and make corrections possible.

There is little in this essay that can be called new. Most of the facts and ideas in it are known by those who are familiar with the literature. Many elements of the plan are found in current programs. What is new, if any novelty can be rightly claimed, is the outline of a systematic and basic plan of teacher education drawn in practical terms. If this essay stimulates others to think in comprehensive terms about the education of the nation's teachers, if it helps to lift teacher education out of the provincialism into which it has drifted and to move it to a sphere commensurate with the demands of these times, it will have served its purpose.

This book had to be completed by a specified time. It would not have been possible to do this had it not been for the encouragement and help of the Institute Task Force and the assistance of a number of persons. Special gratitude must be expressed for the able assistance of Mrs. Esther Hemsing and Miss Martha Bergland. When the manuscript was in its semifinal form, Mrs. Hemsing clarified and refined the discourse at many points, edited it for publication, and saw it through the press. Save for her untiring efforts and diligent attention to significant details, the publication schedule could not have been met. Miss Bergland edited the manuscript in its various stages of development, beginning with the first rough draft and ending with its submission to AACTE. Without her day-to-day editing of the discourse, the manuscript could not have been made ready in the allotted time. Whatever clarity and succinctness the discourse has are to be attributed largely to these two editors.

One of the necessities in the preparation of a manuscript is the accumulation of information on a large number of questions and issues, much of which makes up the margin of knowledge an author needs as a source of security. This information was supplied by three able assistants: Messrs. James Anderson, Norman Smith, and Elmer Wright. Deep appreciation is here expressed for their unstinted help.

Special thanks are due to Miss Judith Hancock, a graduate student at the University of Washington who typed the manuscript again and again as it went through its various stages. The accuracy and speed of her typing, as well as critical comments on various points, added immeasurably to our efforts to complete the work on time.

B. OTHANEL SMITH

February, 1969

CONTENTS

Introduction 1

1 Deprivation, Racism, and Teacher Education 11

2 The Teacher as a Dropout 21

3 Multiple Teacher Roles and Preparation of Aides 31

4 Theoretical Preparation of the Teacher 41

5 The Situational Teaching of Theoretical Knowledge 51

6 An Approach to Systematic Training 67

7 Shaping the Affective Aspects of Teacher Behavior 81

8 The Training Complex 95

9 Subject Matter Preparation of Teachers 111

10 Preparation in Knowledge *About* Subject Matter 125

11 Preparation in the Governance of the Profession 135

12 Teacher Education as Perennial 151

13 Memo on Money and Action 165

Notes 175

Publications 181

Index 183

INTRODUCTION*

No more intolerable condition can be imposed on a human being than to render him useless. Yet one of the most devastating conditions of modern man, uselessness, is the overwhelming plight of the disadvantaged.

Social Complexity and Teacher Education

Complex social organization, increasingly characterized by huge bureaucracies, is one of the realities of today's world. The essence of modern bureaucracy is its depersonalization of decision making, and inflexibility is one of its basic characteristics. Man is increasingly processed by the machine, which treats everyone alike.

Moreover, the world has become dependent on technology. Every aspect of our lives is influenced by a machine or an electronic device. If our automobile breaks down, we can't get to work. If our telephone fails, we are unable to communicate with those vital to our lives. If electric power fails, we are unable to obtain necessary information or our milk sours. Modern American man could not survive if suddenly deprived of his technological supports. A city would starve if no mechanical devices were available to it.

The world we live in is declining in size daily. Through refinements in technology, people are now accessible to each other where not so long ago their remoteness precluded communication. Specialization generates interdependence and calls for cooperation. The

---

*This chapter was prepared by Arthur Pearl, Hobert W. Burns, and Richard L. Foster, members of the NDEA Task Force.

activities of persons halfway around the globe are not only of economic interest but are vital for our survival.

The world we live in is overwhelmingly non-white. By the year 2000, five billion of the six billion people who live on the earth will be non-white. (Non-white is not a precise description of skin color but rather a designation of those people who, until recently, lived under the control of colonial powers.) Political power is growing in the east and the south. Asia, Africa, and South America are the areas of greatest population growth and potential economic development. For the United States these awesome facts mean that we must learn to find an accommodation with the non-white world different from that attempted in the past.

The world we live in is becoming increasingly urban as well. Ninety percent of the more than 300 million persons who will be alive in the United States at the turn of the century will live on one percent of the land. Most employment will be in human services, since this technologically advanced world is proving itself capable of producing more and more goods with fewer and fewer people.

A complex social organization dependent on complicated machinery produces a situation in which even the most productive find it hard to convince themselves of their importance. The poor accurately perceive their uselessness in this kind of social structure. For the first time in history a society is not dependent on unskilled labor to survive; the group which in the past was enslaved and indentured today serves no useful purpose. The disadvantaged, who suffer most under this social structure, at the same time have the least grievance machinery to use against this monolith, bureaucracy.

Segregation, coupled with bureaucracy, blocks communication. It is virtually impossible for blacks and whites to resolve their differences if they never meet to discuss them. The separation of races heightens hostility and increases xenophobia. Clearly, the separation of the races is a problem that teacher training must confront. Segregation has a negative impact on all segments of the society. For the advantaged, segregation furthers racism and class elitism. For the disadvantaged, the effect of segregation is continued impoverishment.

There are many crucial attributes of the emerging world which must be reflected in the preparation of teachers. The key word in education must be relevance. Is the school, and its programs and teachers, resonating with the critical issues of our time? This question must be answered by teacher training institutions.

In the context of social relevance, "white racism" and teacher training must be high-priority issues. At home and abroad racism is a virulent disease which could conceivably lead to our extinction. Racial, class, and ethnic bias can be found in every aspect of current teacher preparation programs. The selection processes militate against the poor and the minority. The program content reflects current prejudices; the methods of instruction coincide with learning styles of the dominant group. Subtle inequalities are reinforced in the institutions of higher learning. Unless there is scrupulous self-appraisal, unless every aspect of teacher training is carefully reviewed, the changes initiated in teacher preparation as a result of the current crises will be, like so many changes which have gone before, "merely differences which make no difference."

The teacher who is not alerted to the devastations of enforced uselessness, segregation, and bureaucratic management is not adequately educated. The teacher who is not prepared to alter through the schools the devastating conditions of enforced uselessness, segregation, and bureaucratic management is not adequately trained.

Educational Goals and the Disadvantaged

Teacher training must begin with the goals of youth education clearly in mind. Without this basis there can be no valid assessment of teaching or teacher preparation.

The goal of education in any society is to empower youth to act in the interests of society. In a free society that goal must be to empower the individual to act in his own interests without intrusion on the rights of other persons. In a complicated interdependent world, education must be the process whereby all citizens acquire such skills, experiences, and understanding as will allow for a wide range of choice in all vital aspects of life.

Everything that is learned in the name of education must be judged by whether there is clearly current or future use of that learning in making choices. Specifically, there are four areas to which education must direct its attention. Students must become well able to:

1. choose, perform, and enjoy a viable vocation,
2. exercise the complicated task of democratic citizenship,
3. engage in culture-carrying activities, and
4. engage in satisfactory inter- and intra-personal relationships.

In the context of these objectives, the disadvantaged can be defined. Perhaps the only meaningful and noncolonial definition of disadvantaged which can be helpful for teacher training is that which relates the conditions of youth to the goals of education.

Disadvantaged youth are denied choice in careers. They possess neither the "credentials" nor the "sponsor" to escape poverty and thus they are relegated to the intolerable choice of a poor job or no job at all.

Disadvantaged youth lack any semblance of political power and are even denied an opportunity to learn how democratic decision making takes place. A point frequently overlooked when disadvantaged youth attempt to resolve grievances by violent and illegal means is that they never have been introduced to the "appropriate measures."

Disadvantaged youth are stigmatized as *culturally* disadvantaged. This designation tends to exclude them from the broader cultural activities and denigrates the culture which they have evolved. The latter is a form of racism and the former is colonialism.

Disadvantaged youth are denied inter- and intra-personal competence. No organism can attain a sense of personal competence if continually confronted with insoluble problems. The only response possible for the individual in such a situation is to become either apathetic or aggressive. The disadvantaged are restricted in the range of social intercourse by segregation and labeled as socially or emotionally disturbed if they protest against the inequity of the situation.

Specifically rejected here is the theory that the disadvantaged state is the consequence of inferior culture, an inferior socialization by inadequate parents, a stifling of cognitive stimulation in the preschool years, or an inferior intellectual endowment. Acceptance of such "theories" has increased racism and only worsened the situation for the disadvantaged. Teachers must be trained to respect the potential strengths of the disadvantaged rather than be armed with a set of mythologies, masquerading as theories of social science, which only discourage the economically disadvantaged or minority youth from investing in education.

Career choice is vital for disadvantaged youth. Most work now requires many years of formal education, for even the lowest rung on the career ladder. A technologically sophisticated society requires a technologicially sophisticated work force.

If the disadvantaged are to enjoy options in the world of work they must be kept academically alive. They cannot be shunted aside into low ability groups and not allowed to develop the basic skills required further up the educational line. They cannot be shunted into noncollege preparatory tracks which do little more than prepare them for menial jobs. They cannot be isolated by putting them in special classes for the socially and emotionally disturbed. They must not only be kept alive, they must also be given the knowledge and the experience requisite to intelligent choice.

If vocational counseling is to be of value to the disadvantaged, the teacher must become more aware of the nature of the world of work. Among other things, teachers must be encouraged to examine the "credential process" in the largest and fastest growing of all industries—education. It is necessary, in preparing youth for work, to alter the world of work to fit the individual. Nowhere can this be better done than in education. Opening up hundreds of thousands of careers in education to the disadvantaged would increase the choices to the poor and alter the colonialism of the current system.

Both the advantaged and disadvantaged need to be educated to appreciate the importance of democratic institutions. If the advantaged had been properly educated in the essence of democracy, perhaps there would be no disadvantaged. Underpinning all democratic institutions are guaranteed individual rights. As a rule, teachers are not specifically taught to respect the rights of individuals. The poor, the black, the Indian, and the Mexican are all too often denied even a semblance of guaranteed elemental rights.

Basic to every school and the education of every teacher is a thorough grounding in the due process of the law, the assumption of innocence until proof "beyond reasonable doubt" establishes guilt, protection against cruel and unusual punishments, freedom of expression, freedom to challenge authority without fear of reprisal.

But teacher preparation must go beyond instilling a devotion to human rights. It must also include those things which would enable prospective teachers to help children and youth assume the responsibilities of democratic citizenship, such as the ability to exercise intelligent choice in the selection of persons for legislative, executive, and judicial decision making. Only when student government deals with such realities as control over money, determination of rules, a voice in the curriculum, and some power in selection and retention of teachers, and only when these activities are available to all students, will student government be part of the developing process which leads to an enlightened electorate.

Modern man needs to be intellectually voracious to survive. He must learn the lessons of history. The nature of his complex interrelationships requires more proficiency in communication and technological skills than was demanded in the past. He must, to maintain his sanity, be able to enjoy art, music, and literature. These culture-carrying activities would appear to be emphasized in the curriculum; yet even superficial examination shows this not to be true. There is very little excitement in the school for anyone: the poorer one is, the drearier his school experience.[1]

And dreariness is not the worst characteristic of the school. Much worse are the instances of teachers who reinforce racism. In some cases they are blatant and overt racists, but more frequently they are guilty of omission and insensitivity. Teachers tend to confuse race, class, and ethnic bias with academic standards. Nowhere is this truer than in the study of language. Teachers, by limited experience and specialized training, consider their language the only acceptable code. They confuse provincialism with scholarship. They fail to appreciate what Emerson noted 130 years ago: "Colleges and books only copy the language which the field and work-house made."[2]

If a student is told his language is inferior, then everything which depends on language is tainted. The language of black students is judged without even asking why they developed their own style of communication. One need not go as far as Emerson, who wrote:

"Everyone has felt how superior in force is the language of the street to that of the academy. . . the speech of the man in the street is invariably strong, nor can you mend it by making it what you call parliamentary. . . The power of their speech is that it is perfectly understood by all. . . (it) is always strong. Cut these words and they would bleed; they are vascular and alive; they walk and run. Moreover they who speak them have this elegancy, they do not trip in their speech. It is a shower of bullets, whilst Cambridge men and Yale men correct themselves and begin again at every half sentence."[3]

But it is imperative to respect the various languages as equal and to develop a common code from the best of all that is spoken rather than impose on all arbitrarily a "standard code."

What passes for instruction in history typically suffers from omission and distortion: the evils of slavery are mitigated, the genocidal wars against Indian nations are played down, and the wars of aggression against Mexico are denied. Is it any wonder that blacks, Mexicans, and Indians become disengaged from a process where engagement would require the acceptance of insult and slur? It is not enough to extirpate racism. It is necessary to develop pride in social identity. The establishment of Afro-American study centers, Mexican study centers, and Indian study centers is vital for the establishment of "race" pride in those whom history has treated shabbily. But such centers are equally necessary for the education of the affluent white whose survival in an essentially non-white world depends on the eradication of every vestige of white supremacy.

Man must learn to live with himself and his neighbors. Excluding all who are different is no solution. Segregating by race and class is no solution. To stand aside while a college student commits suicide (every ninety minutes a college student dies by his own hand) is no solution. To proclaim futilely that psychoactive agents are illegal, while more and more young people become dependent on such things, is no solution. A school designed to resolve racial antagonisms within the school *can* lead to a reduction in the number of racists. (Today, when disturbances break out, students are suspended or the school is closed.) Only when the school reaches out to the lonely, when it respects the right of individuals to be different, and facilitates the socialization of the antisocial will it be doing a good job. And that can happen only when teachers are trained to deal with such problems.

The Attributes of Effective Teachers

The essential thesis of these pages is that a revitalization of education must take place if this nation is to survive. If a school system is to function effectively, it needs the staff to match its mountainous problems. The situation as it exists now is not only inadequate, it holds the seeds of our destruction.

If a major problem of modern man is how to cope with depersonalization, then it is essential that a teacher be human. If a student is to be prepared for the evolving world, then an essential attribute of the effective teacher is awareness of the realities of that world. If modern man suffers from intolerable feelings of uselessness, then the teacher must be able to structure and supervise situations where men can engage in useful activities. If estrangement of the races and the classes is a major problem, then the teacher must have the skill to bring persons of different races and classes together and to keep the communication process going until differences are resolved. If the problems of tomorrow are to be understood by learning the lessons of yesterday, then the teacher must be well versed in history. If art and music are means by which complicated messages are communicated, the teacher needs to be well versed in these too.

The teacher must be prepared to negotiate interpersonal contracts with students. The effective teacher is a person the student trusts. Only a student can discover if the teacher is trustworthy. Therefore, in the training and the evaluation of the trainee's performance, his pupils should be used as a source of data.

The teacher must share valuable knowledge and experience. To do this, he must show the student that what he has to offer is valuable. Also, the teacher must have that which he is asked to share. To teach reading the teacher must know reading. To teach history the teacher must be immersed in history. It is no overstatement that teacher preparation institutions are willing to certify persons prepared to teach who have but a small amount of knowledge and even less commitment to scholarly endeavor.

The teacher must know how to communicate to broad segments of the society. At present many pupils are victimized because the teacher is unable to speak their language. Recruitment of teachers primarily from middle income populations contributes to the problems of communication. Teacher preparation further restricts the communication process. Alienation of youth from adult establishments only highlights the difficulty. Teacher preparation must include sensitizing to a variety of legitimate languages. A teacher who is ignorant of linguistics is not a good teacher, no matter what his area of competence.

The teacher must be able to understand the student's world. Teachers currently build barriers between themselves and students because they have been provided with inadequate theory and outmoded concepts. Students are eager to learn, and they cease to grow only when informed that they are intellectually incompetent, not useful to the classroom, and intruders into the educational process. Many teachers willingly and witlessly deliver such messages daily because that is what they are trained to do.

Here, too, the disadvantaged are dealt with most cruelly. Because of ignorance the teacher is likely to confuse unintelligibility of curriculum with lack of intelligence of students. Because of remoteness from the life of the disadvantaged, the teacher is likely to make the pupil feel unwelcome in the school and then convince himself that this is evidence the pupil doesn't want to learn. Because the teacher is unable to assess the extent to which class, race, and ethnic bias have influenced his perceptions, he is likely to confuse a response to such aggressions as evidence of a student's inability to maintain self-control.

Some social scientists have put forth biased conclusions under the guise of science. They have not sorted out cause from effect and have fortified the teacher with "scientific support" for racial and class prejudice. No teacher with such prejudices and no teacher training institution which contributes to the development of such prejudices can claim to be doing its job. Institutions of higher learning are funded to educate teachers to work with disadvantaged youth yet are rarely examined for the underlying social basis of their programs. Often the schools which themselves helped generate and reinforce the original social prejudices are asked to reform the teacher.

Repair, Reform, or Revolution?

This work calls for change in education generally, and specifically, for changes in training persons to be teachers. There is lamentably little recognition of the crisis in education. There is smugness where there should be concern; complaining "jams" the few voices urging true innovation and change. The moderate and the mild control the destiny of education. They have deluded themselves that blunted emotions signify maturity. They desire change but the change is only some modest tinkering. They wish to repair the system by replacing worn-out parts. In training teachers to work with the disadvantaged they may add a course or two, or bring to the faculty a person who claims expertness in this area. All too often the instructional program reinforces the notion of cultural deprivation and as such may be a negative rather than a positive influence on the teacher.

Education is beyond repair! What is needed is radical *reform.* This reform is to include the nature of the schooling process, the systems which control educational policy, and the institutions which prepare persons to be teachers. In teacher training, reform must be undertaken in the selection of teachers. There must be more adequate representation of the poor, the black, the Mexican, and the Indian in teaching ranks.

The current situation of remoteness of the prospective teacher from the realities of classroom practice must be reformed. Prospective teachers must be brought into contact with reality through various training experiences and actual encounters with children in the classroom.

Anti-intellectualism of teachers can no longer be condoned. The reform of teacher education must be to further scholarship. Teachers must become avid readers consumed by history and by language, conversant with scientific principles, and at home with mathematical manipulations.

The schools must allow persons with different capacities to function where they can be most useful. Teachers must be specifically trained for different positions in a program which recognizes the importance of a differentiated staff.

Teacher preparation reform must stress the ability to conceptualize and analyze, which is the essence of scholarship. The teacher must be prepared not only to diagnose problems, but also to devise programs to remedy the situation, and finally to evaluate the success of these programs.

Nothing short of these reforms will suffice.

Reform is distinguished from revolution. It is not assumed that reform will require a complete transfer of power. But in the absence of revolution, reform in control over education must take place. There must be some sharing of power with community leaders, teachers, and students. The reform must recognize the plurality of our society.

Today, the alternative to reform is revolution. With revolution there is a complete exchange of power. In teacher education this would mean that those who currently control the education of teachers would be overthrown. The authors do not believe there is now a revolutionary potential and are persuaded that reform measures could bring about those changes which are necessary. However, there are ominous signs of revolution: the black insistence on control of local schools, student resistance to control on the campus, and heightened teacher militancy. Heightened resistance of taxpayers, reluctance of suburbanites to cooperate with moves toward integration, and political success of simplistic slogans like "return to fundamentals" are warnings from the other camp. To ignore these warnings is to court disaster.

Funding Strategies and the Possibility of Reform

Changes in teacher training will eventually depend upon funding policies and strategy. The Education Professions Development Act can be a means of producing change. The legislative intent was clearly influenced by social imperatives. The guidelines reflect the urgencies of our time. But more is needed—the kinds of programs to be funded must also be specified.

It is not expected that revolutionary programs will receive support. Governments do not fund programs to overthrow themselves. But programs which purport to repair may be supported and this would be a tragic mistake. In times of precious few resources, when much must be done and there is far too little with which to do it, waste becomes the greatest enemy. The Office of Education and other funding resources have to muster the courage to back the courageous.

We urge that only those teacher training programs which relate directly to the primary issues of our time be funded.

We urge that only reform programs that entail cooperation of the community, the teachers, the local and state administration, and the institutions of higher education be funded.

We urge that only those programs that deal directly with elimination of "white racism" and the alienation of youth from adult institutions be funded.

CHAPTER 1

DEPRIVATION, RACISM, AND TEACHER EDUCATION

American society is a mixture of national origins and social classes. In some schools as many as fifty nationalities are represented in the pupil body. Because of local conditions and pressures to integrate the schools, children of the poor and the wealthy, the illiterate and the educated, are sometimes found in the same school. But in the inner city the Negroes and the Puerto Ricans are forced by circumstance to live off by themselves, and thus their children attend schools in which there is less variation of cultural background and wealth. The same observation can be made about the children who live in rural poverty, or in Mexican communities, or on Indian reservations. Such variety among communities and pupils demands that all educational personnel be prepared to cope with problems arising from all kinds of social circumstances.

Even where the children come from apparently similar social and racial situations, as in suburbia or the black ghettos, a teacher ought to have a broad background, not only better to understand a child's situation but to direct him in his search for broader experiences. For example, a teacher who knows that use of a dialect is in itself no indication of shallowness of thought or feeling may be able to relate to the child by showing an understanding of the depth and vigor of that dialect. From this the teacher may expand the ability of the child to use language in a way that helps him maintain respect for both his old and new manners of speech. To extend his language habits is to expand the child's possibilities of human associations.

But instead of preparing teachers to be at ease with children of any social origin, the colleges are typically preparing teachers for children who are much like themselves. Even for these the prepara-

tion is inadequate, since these children themselves are stunted if
they are not helped to understand other kinds of people. Awareness
of this significant discovery has finally led federal, state, and local
authorities to emphasize the preparation of teachers for those
children who live in poor economic circumstances.

Should teachers for culturally deprived children be given some
special type of training as are the teachers of the blind or mentally
handicapped? One answer to this question is that the special motivations, attitudes, language system, and conduct of disadvantaged
children require that their teachers be trained in methods different
from teachers of middle class children. Another answer is that underprivileged children learn in the same way as other children and that
their teachers need no special training. This latter is the view taken
here. The problem of preparing teachers adequately for the disadvantaged is the same as the problem of preparing teachers adequately for all children. We do not need special teachers for the
children of different ethnic and social groups. Rather, we need
teachers who are able to work effectively with children regardless
of race or social situation, but mindful of what that is in each case.

The special circumstances from which children come cannot,
indeed, be ignored in the preparation of teachers. On the contrary,
teachers should be trained to work with the cultural and racial background of each child. A child's cultural heritage should be considered by his teacher to be the basis for his education, not a
stumbling block. A child should learn because of what he already
knows, not in spite of it. "Culturally deprived" is not an accurate
term. No one is lacking in culture whether he be from the vast
ranks of the poor, or the middle or upper class, or from differing
areas of the country. The poor are not lacking in culture; theirs is as
different from that of the middle class as the Southern culture is
different from the New England culture. For example, one of the
authors of *The Disadvantaged: Challenge to Education* speaks of
interesting an eighth grade class in poetry. The teacher presented
them a poem by Langston Hughes written in a dialect close to their
own and known in Hughes' time as "jive." The class came alive and
participated as any good teacher dreams of his class doing, illustrating
"an approach to nonstandard dialect in such a way that the pupils
feel that learning standard English dialect doesn't mean that they
must discard their own."[1]

The teaching of poor children does not require unique skills, as
does teaching the blind, for the handicap comes not from the children
themselves but is placed upon them by the situations in which they
live and the schools to which they go. But it does require broad
life experiences which few middle class teachers have had. Unless we
stress this view of teacher education, we can unintentionally aggravate

a potentially explosive division between the social classes and ethnic groups in our society.

False Ideas about the Disadvantaged

So much has been written and said about the extreme want and educational starvation of these children that a false image has been created. It is easy to imagine that they are somehow emotionally and intellectually inferior. These children are basically the same as all other children. Though their experience may be different, they too are interested in their world, attached to their families, and have important hopes and aspirations. If these characteristics are not visible to their teachers, it is because the teachers see only with the narrow vision of the middle class.

Another false image of deprived children is that they are all alike. In truth they are as different from one another as the children of other elements of the population. The poor are different in life styles: the Appalachian white child, the Mexican child, the Negro child and the Indian child have distinct outlooks and modes of behavior,[2] although the differences within these groups are as large as the differences among them. The black youth of the ghetto is greatly influenced, often controlled, by the norms and power of his peer group. The Appalachian youth is influenced more by his family and the adult community. Like the youth of the ghetto, he also is inclined to be resourceful and independent. The Mexican-American so closely identifies with his family and its cultural milieu that he is often more at variance with the norms of the school than either the Appalachian white or the Negro of the ghetto. The Indian child lives in a culture almost entirely apart from the culture of the white man or Appalachian, Mexican, or Negro variations.

If one considers affluent children, he will find differences among them as striking as those among the poor. There will be physical as well as cultural differences attributable to social origins, occupations of their parents, and family income. Many children of the very affluent have had a great deal of experience at sophisticated levels. To them school is apt to be dull and lack the sensational experiences to which they are accustomed. The children of the families from skilled occupations and proprietary groups are apt to be ambitious, although they do not always pursue the knowledge that could fulfill their ambitions. These are rather gross distinctions and in some cases they will not hold. But they will suggest the differences that often seem unexpectedly great to teachers moving from a "comfortable" school to a different one.

If we look again at disadvantaged children, we see that some of them come from families which are chronically poor.[3] These people live on the barest necessities of life and are for the most part

14

demoralized and hopeless. Many live in filth and degradation and would perish without some form of public aid. At this level of cultural existence children see little in the future except the kind of life their parents have had. The schools appear to offer them neither hope nor learning. For this hard core, poverty is a way of life.

Economically-, socially-, and educationally-disadvantaged children are not new to American society. Throughout American history since colonial days, disadvantaged youths and their families have made heroic efforts to avail themselves of schools. The existence of the free public school system itself can be attributed largely to the struggle of the laboring man to provide an education for his children. Even though the public school system is now well fixed in the American institutional structure, the struggle for an adequate program of education for the children of low income groups continues.

Disadvantages and Deprivations*

It is futile to look at the disadvantaged as a homogeneous group. What is emerging from the mass of literature on the deprived is that it is more profitable, certainly for pedagogical purposes, to look at the social and economic factors which cause problems for children in relation to the school.

One of the central conditions which affects many disadvantaged schoolchildren is simply lack of money. Many studies indicate that the cost of schooling (dues, trips, out-of-pocket expense, collections for various causes, loss of family income, etc.) places an undue hardship on the child whose family is poor. If school is expensive, the child who cannot afford the cost of schooling must either avoid the cost and not participate in the school's program or accept the charity of the school. Either route is unacceptable. If the child does not participate, his experience is limited and his self-esteem may be damaged. If he accepts the charity of the school, the injury to his self-concept is apt to be even greater. For, as the Webbs pointed out long ago, charity degrades both the giver and the receiver.

The children of poverty suffer chronically from malnutrition. Depression, apathy, limited amounts of energy, and lethargy are but some of the effects of poor nutrition. The impact of malnutrition on the functioning of the child in school indicates the close interrelation between the school and community life of the child. The hunger which a child carries to school lessens his performance and affects his attitudes.

The disadvantaged child is often affected adversely by the instability of his family and the unemployment of his parents. There is considerable evidence showing the close connection between the

* This section was prepared by Vernon Haubrich, College of Education, University of Wisconsin.

degree of family stability and the child's ability to profit from schooling. It is very difficult in school for a child who comes from a home that is broken but has economic security, but it is almost devastating for one who comes from a home where there is neither family nor economic stability.

One of the conditions which induces a sense of futility among the disadvantaged is the failure of the helping professions to perform their tasks adequately among the poor whites, the black, the Indian, and the migrant. Legal services for these people are almost non-existent. The record of police discrimination is one of the salient features of the Kerner Report. Medical services are often unavailable to the poor, causing some groups to forfeit, on the average, as much as a quarter of a century of their lives. The failure of the medical profession to respond to the needs of the poor stems partly from a desire to be compensated for services rendered, but it is also a commentary on the nature of our social priorities: profit is placed above service where people are concerned. The lack of response of psychiatrists and psychologists to the needs of the poor is notorious. Similar examples document the failure of human services to meet social responsibilities and show the classic bias that is built into our social system.

The massive evidence which has been assembled to document the plight of the Negro shows only too well the prejudices of the white man and the effects of racial discrimination upon black children. The recent Racial Isolation Report, the Coleman Report, and the Kerner Report add weight to years of scholarly findings and indicate the immense impact of segregation on the black children of society. Segregation has created in many Negro children a sense of inferiority, a negative self-image, and a feeling that blackness is a stigma.

When one takes all of these facts into account, the failure of deprived children to respond to traditional programs of schooling is understandable. Yet some conclude that the children's serious environmental deficits make adjusting to the work of the school impossible. Others believe that the curriculum, teachers, and school organization simply cannot be adapted to the uniquenesses of disadvantaged children. The blame can be placed on the child or on the school. But the fact of the school's ineffectiveness remains. The disadvantaged child seems to get progressively further behind in his achievement, in his adjustment to the demands of schooling, and in his relationships to teachers.

The school system itself is one of the conditions that accentuates the problems of the deprived child. Recent evidence from the disadvantaged themselves, in the Kerner Report, indicates that the school is not as high on the list of complaints as other social agencies. Still, the teaching profession would be foolish to ignore evidence in dropout rates, comparative scores on tests, turnover of teachers in poor and ghetto areas, and other measurements indicating a pattern of discrimination to which the schools wittingly or unwittingly contribute.

If the education of the teacher is looked at in the context of the great variation among the children of the American people, the enormous dimensions of the teacher's task become only too clear. The educational system, no less than the American people, is devoted to the idea of a common school. It is the only institution through which all the children of all the people share in the wide range of experience that is both the richness and the poverty of American life. The teacher who can work with the children of only one social stratum or minority group is inadequately prepared to teach in the common school. The idea that the backgrounds and interests of the child must be understood if he is to be properly taught must now be put into practice. Furthermore, skills and techniques of effective interaction with children and adults at all points on the social spectrum must be built into the competency of every teacher.

The Disadvantaged and Racism

The problem of educating disadvantaged children can too easily become confused with the problems caused by the white man's prejudice and discriminations against the black man. The disadvantaged child is a product of his social class, and his deficiencies are attributable to the race of his parents only to the extent that white prejudice creates their poverty and other environmental limitations. The problem of educating the deprived child would exist if the total population of the country were either entirely white or entirely black. To be disadvantaged is to be a member of the lower social class, regardless of race or minority group.

Educational and economic deprivation is drastically increased by the existence of racism. Racism would deny an individual, because of color, the privilege of living in any part of the community he prefers, of being buried in any spot of earth he can afford, of holding a job for which he is fully competent, of getting an adequate education, and of associating freely with his friends regardless of their race.

Human beings have always set themselves apart from others on the dogma that some are by nature superior. This dogma was used as the justification of all forms of slavery, and, while a great proportion of the peoples of the earth have discarded it legally, there are still many who hold to it tenaciously. This dogma is the ultimate rationalization of the militant white when he is forced to justify his discriminations and crimes against the Negro. He may not say it in so many words, but what he means is that, by nature, the blood of the white is superior to that of the black.

In racism, not only is the total group discriminated against, but the individual must carry the injustices which the white man's prejudices place upon the group. No matter how well the Negro may be educated or how wealthy he may be, the racist considers him to be inferior and enforces this belief in a thousand ways frequently too subtle to be perceived. In a democracy it is by the principle of achievement that the social position of an individual should be determined, not by his blood or his wealth. In actual practice, however, achievement has been combined with wealth. Racism has denied even the nation's most famous Negroes the respect to which they were entitled by achievement.

The condemnation of the total group because of blood is the dogma of racial superiority that underlay Nazism. The basic idea of Nazism was not that the state is superior to the individual, but that the state is the instrument of the superior race in its efforts to reconstruct the world in its own image. In this sense, white prejudice in this country is much like the doctrine of racial superiority of the Nazi movement.

The Negro is not in the ghettos by his own choice. He is not in the work camps and the rural slums of the South because he wants to be there. He is in these places because that is where racist discriminations have placed him. The Irish once populated the ghettos Negroes occupy today. The Italians and Jews also lived there. These people had their own schools, policemen, commercial enterprises, and small shops. In time they accumulated enough wealth and education to move out of the inner city to places more comfortable to live and rear children.

In these earlier ghettos there were were jobs, industries, strong traditions, and morale to nourish and sustain the individual. But there are no jobs, no enterprises, and few traditions in the black ghettos, only hopelessness and loss of identity. The Negro has not been able to better himself while in the ghetto and to enjoy social mobility because American society is closed to him in countless ways. A great deal is said about our "open" society, but what we overlook is that it is open differentially to people according to their economic status and color. No one wishes to condemn the ideology of an open society just because American society at this point in its history is not completely open. It is the ideal by which men live and struggle to improve their social institutions and practices. The ideology must not be used to gloss over the hard fact that the ideal has yet to be realized.

As long as the political bureaucracies of the cities discriminate against the Negro in the appointment of police and teachers and in providing social services, and just as long as the financial system discriminates against the Negro by not giving him loans for business and housing, as long as real estate interests are able to build boundaries around the Negro by zoning and other means of exclusion, just that long will the ghettos continue to exist. The white man's hostility is deplorable enough, but even worse than hostility is his insidious patronage and discrimination in education, employment, and business, and in countless other ways.

Social Integration and the Schools

In recent years a great deal has been written about apartheid in South Africa. Actually it is only the word that is new in American culture. Segregation and political and economic discrimination against the black man have existed here for over 350 years, and until recently they were reinforced by legal enactments and court decisions. The legal and judicial barriers to racial integration are being reduced. Eventually white prejudice may begin to erode, and the time may not be too distant when many of the worst features of racial discrimination will be wiped out.

But at the very time when the nation is moving toward the elimination of its legal and judicial impediments to an open society, some black militants are moving to close ranks and to insist upon separation. Social change always lags far behind the promises and hopes of men. The suffering in the ghettos and in the rural slums of the South is intolerable to a self-respecting people who constantly find their hopes and efforts to improve their lot thwarted by the prejudices and discriminations of the whites. But democracy cannot continue to survive in a society that follows a policy of segregation and isolation of its races. The very essence of democracy is that men are equal one to another and that this equality can be honored only in unfettered human association. Were the white militants who favor a doctrine of apartheid and the black militants who follow a separatist doctrine to succeed, the ideal of democracy in this country would perish. There would then be no guides left for those who criticize society and work for its improvement.

Social integration is a means and a goal. As a means, it is a partial solution to problems created by white prejudice. As a goal, effectively achieved, it is a true sign that massive prejudice has been eliminated. So it is with school integration. But a token integration of the schools is hardly more than a gesture.

School integration is more fundamental than the mere mingling of different races in a school building. Integration is the incorporation of individuals of different races as equals into a social group. Furthermore, school integration involves the hierarchical system by which the schools are administered and education carried on.

Malcolm X pointed out several years ago that school segregation meant not only the separation of the races into different buildings but also the control of the Negro schools by the white power group.[4] He went on to point out that integration simply brought the black and white children together and left the white power structure in control. At that time, he was arguing for black schools under black control. There is nothing undemocratic about a community predominantly Negro which exercises control over its schools in the same sense that a community predominantly white or upper middle class exercises control over its schools. As long as social and economic integration is denied the Negro there is no reason to deny him the privilege of managing the affairs which affect his life. No group can run the affairs of another without debilitating it. Human development depends upon the involvement of the individual in the affairs that concern him. The right of the Negro to participate in his own affairs cannot on any moral principle be denied. If integration of the schools is to occur, it must involve the participation of the Negro in the control and management of the schools as well as the classrooms.

Because of discrimination in business and housing, and lack of other human consideration, it may be many years before the black ghettos are dissolved or integrated. In the meantime, school integration must be pursued as vigorously as possible. When black and white children are bussed into mixed classes of high quality, both groups gain from the experience. The moving of Negro children into schools that are predominantly white and a corresponding transporting of white pupils into schools that are predominantly black must be increased so that larger, meaningful numbers are involved. But two-way movement is in and of itself insufficient. It is a step toward integration, not integration in its social and psychological sense.

Teacher Preparation and School Integration

The problem of training teachers for schools in disadvantaged areas is not the same as the problem of preparing teachers to deal with racism in school and society. The teacher may be well prepared to work with children and parents who are victims of economic and social deprivation. He may know how to relate to them, to empathize with them, and he may understand quite fully the social and economic forces that cause their plight. He may correctly assess the experiential background of the children and tailor his instruction to their interests and needs. He may know what sort of content is most conducive to their development and he may know how to handle that content intellectually and with technological devices. He may know all of these things and still be baffled by the problems in an integrated school which originate in racism.

He may not know how to handle discipline problems in a racially mixed group, especially if part of the group is from a culturally deprived area. If a Negro teacher is confronted by discipline problems with a white child in his classroom, the problem may be much more serious to him than the same conduct would be with a Negro child. He may be concerned with the reaction of the white parents, as well as the child, to the steps he takes. The same can be said of the white teacher who has an integrated class. In some integrated schools, communication between the white and the black pupils is either nonexistent or has largely broken down. The problem of restoring communication in such a situation is one with which the whole school faculty must struggle.

The teacher must also face the question of racial prejudice in himself. The white teacher harbors many prejudices of which he is unaware. The Negro teacher may carry feelings of resentment and aggression that come with a feeling of imposed inferiority. It is necessary for the teacher to face his personal problems squarely and to include in his program of preparation experiences to shock him into the realization of his prejudices and show him how to deal with them. Just as there are prejudices in the teacher's feelings and modes of thought, so too are these to be found in pupils and in the adults of the community.

Proper education of the teacher will lead him to examine his own human prejudices generally and, specifically, his racial prejudices, and it will discipline him in the techniques of handling problems of interpersonal relations that arise from racial prejudices in his students and their parents.

CHAPTER 2

THE TEACHER AS A DROPOUT

There are at least two sides to the staffing of the school system: the recruitment and preparation of teachers, and their further training and retention once they are employed. The problem of staffing middle class and affluent schools is essentially the same as that of providing teachers for the schools of the disadvantaged. There are differences, though not basic, which are genuine and demand special consideration. The attrition of the teaching personnel in deprived areas is due not only to the constant exodus of teachers from the profession generally but to the particular combination of circumstances which confronts the teacher in the deprived communities.

Ironically, teachers too can be dropouts from the schools in which they teach and from their profession. The rate at which they leave is disconcerting and has received much less attention than that of pupil dropout, although the influences that drive the teacher from the classroom may also contribute to pupil withdrawals.

The special problem of staffing schools in disadvantaged areas is best understood in the context of the national supply and demand of teachers, and the forces that influence the individual to remain in the profession. In 1967, about 227,000 persons completed teacher education programs with either a bachelor's or a master's degree.[1] The number of new teachers, not including aides and other personnel, needed to provide the nation's children with a minimum level of quality education was estimated at 384,000, or roughly 160,000 more than were actually produced.[2] However, the real situation is even more disconcerting because only about 165,000 of those who completed teacher education programs actually entered teaching when they were graduated, a loss of some 62,000. A little more than 70 percent of the teachers who are prepared each year do, in fact, become immediately employed in the school system. This proportion has been nearly constant for the last decade.

What happens to those who do not enter teaching? A survey of the occupational distribution of persons who completed teacher education programs from September, 1965 to August, 1966 shows that about 5 percent went into other gainful occupations, about 6 percent continued their schooling, approximately 3 percent became homemakers, and less than 2 percent entered the military. Some 13 percent were not accounted for.[3] Some of those who drop out at the time they finish their preparation will later return. This is especially true of women who marry as soon as they are graduated, for many of them will teach when their children are grown.

Moreover, about 12 percent of all teachers leave the schools at the end of each school year. Some of these will come back, especially women who drop out to rear their children. They begin to return to the classrooms between the ages of 35 and 39, and the highest proportion of them return between the ages of 40 and 49.[4]

A word may be in order here about components of the teaching force. In 1960, the last year for which complete census data are available, the total number of men teaching in the public schools was 419,528. Of these, 30,597, or about 7 percent, were Negro men. The Negro men teachers were equally divided between the elementary grades and the high school. In the same year there were 101,512 Negro women teachers out of a total of 1,111,721, or about 9 percent. Almost 82,000 of these Negro women teachers were in the elementary school, and 19,567 were in the high school. Altogether there were 132,109 Negro teachers in the elementary and high schools. This is approximately 9 percent of the total number of teachers who taught in the public schools in 1960.[5] This proportion of Negro teachers to whites is roughly in the same ratio as the proportion of blacks to whites in the country as a whole.

According to the Coleman Report, the average white elementary pupil attends a school in which 97 percent of the teachers are white. On the other hand, the average black elementary pupil attends a school where 65 percent of the teachers are black. This racial distribution of teachers will, of course, be remedied only if a policy of personnel integration is carried out along with the integration of the pupil body.

Why Teachers Drop Out

One may well ask why people leave any occupation, for no calling is without some attrition. But the rate of withdrawal from the teaching profession is excessive compared to other college-based occupations such as medicine, pharmacy, and law. This fact, together with the shortage of teachers and the amount of time and energy given to their preparation, makes the question of teacher dropouts particularly important. While the mobility and exodus of teachers has been investigated, only the demography of the teaching profession yields hard evidence. The *explanation* of the demographic facts remains at best speculative.

Discerning the motivation for entering teaching is a complex and vague process. Probably the teachers themselves cannot honestly pinpoint one reason for their decision to teach. It is likely that there are many indistinguishable reasons for each decision. Nevertheless it is widely believed on sociological grounds that individuals who enter teaching with ulterior motives are unlikely to remain in the teaching field.

It is often said that those who enter teaching are socially ambitious and that they stay with teaching only as long as they can use it as a step to something better. Part of the evidence in support of this thesis is that approximately 80 percent of the teaching force is recruited from the middle class and that a good proportion of this percentage comes from the lower middle class. The remaining 20 percent comes from the upper layer of the lower class. The lower middle class and the upper lower class are the most ambitious parts of the population. Unlike the upper class which has arrived and the lower class which has little hope, the people who come from these social strata are on the move. So, according to this argument, the exodus from the profession and the mobility within it arise from the aspirations of those who enter it. Their ambition is more for a higher social than economic status, though these certainly are interrelated. Of course, the economic factor could be more potent were it increased. If teachers were paid as much again as they now receive, they would be less inclined to drop out. The middle and lower classes contain a considerable proportion of teachers who use teaching as a stepping stone to more lucrative occupations or to marriage into families above them socially. Despite the plausibility of this notion, three-fourths of the teachers say that they would choose teaching as a career were they given the chance to start over again.[6] They tend to find most satisfaction in their pupils, and the feeling of satisfaction in their career choice is higher among women than men. A greater degree of dissatisfaction among men teachers may arise from comparing themselves with men in other occupations who enjoy higher incomes and greater prestige. The women, on the other hand, often find that other occupations actually open to them pay less and have less prestige than teaching.

While the desire for upward social mobility may account for a number of individuals leaving the teaching field, it does not explain why a large proportion of those trained to teach do not feel committed enough to enter teaching in the first place. Some, especially men, never teach because they find better paying jobs in related fields. Many women who have prepared themselves to teach marry as soon as they are graduated. Perhaps the main reason that so many trained teachers never enter the classroom is a lack of commitment to the profession born of little investment in preparation for it. Not many people who are prepared to practice medicine or law fail to follow their profession; in all probability they would consider their failure to practice a waste of knowledge and training. Apparently those who are prepared to teach but never enter the classroom do not feel this sense of waste. Perhaps they feel that the amount of knowledge wasted is not that great or that valuable. If physicians were trained by giving them only basic liberal arts and science courses and four or five courses in medicine in the junior and senior years, perhaps they would not feel committed to their vocations or competent to practice. Yet this is the way teachers are now trained. They are given a basic liberal arts program covered over with a thin veneer of pedagogy. If they change their occupational goals and decide to abandon teaching before they enter it, they have lost practically nothing since their preparation is essentially the same as that of a liberal arts graduate. If the teacher were required to make a heavy investment in preparation, he would either not enter the field in the first place or not drop out.

A professional person is trained for and dedicated to the performance of a set of tasks within a flexible theoretical framework. But programs of teacher preparation equip the prospective teacher to perform very few specific tasks and to understand only superficially the situations he must deal with as a teacher. Indeed, he acquires a blurred image of the teacher's role and of its potentialities for social service. The occupation is fraught with the good of humanity. It contains much that is inspiring, but it is neither an easy occupation nor one that reflects a romantic past. Like other professions, it entails routine work punctuated by challenging problems. Inspiration can carry the teacher to heights of success only if he has the proper preparation. But without it inspiration is apt to be futile. Only if teachers are prepared as professionals are they apt to act like dedicated individuals. Some teachers never take up their profession because they realize that they are not sufficiently trained for the job.

It is believed also that the beginning teacher loses interest in his work and drops out because of the circumstances in which he is placed. He is sometimes given a heavier load than experienced teachers and is usually given the poorest choice of assignments because of the seniority system which operates in many schools, especially in large systems. In particular, the beginning teacher is often burdened with clerical duties and extraclassroom assignments such as hall and bus duties, study hall responsibilities, and lunchroom supervision. All of these sap his energies and consume his time. The beginner is typically given little help on the problems that he faces because the experienced teachers are too busy to assist him or the supervisory staff of the school system is inadequate. So the beginning teacher often works in a professional vacuum without any reference standard against which to judge his performance. If he finds himself overwhelmed by discipline problems or lack of adequate rapport with his pupils, he may benefit from assistance from experienced teachers who have dealt successfully with such difficulties. A teacher who is having trouble relating to his pupils and handling the materials of instruction needs the support and advice of established teachers. But all too often the school system makes no provision for such assistance.

The bewildering network of activities into which the beginning teacher is drawn often confuses him and leads him to wonder what the role of a teacher actually is. In many instances he loses sight of his responsibility for educating his pupils as he attempts to meet and deal with all the influences that play upon him from one hour to the next. The natural tendency of an individual in such circumstances is to flee at the earliest opportunity.

The individual who sticks it out for the first year or two and begins to assume the role of a career teacher continues to be burdened with extraclassroom responsibilities and often with classroom problems with which he has been unable to cope. Somehow he manages to make adjustments to these only to find that while he may try to conduct himself as a professional he is not treated as such. Whatever else may be characteristic of a professional worker, one thing is certain: he is entitled to make decisions that pertain to his work and to participate in the making of policies respecting the conditions of his labor. In fact, these are the ordinary rights expected by any artisan or professionally trained person. But the teacher is too often denied the privileges which the artisan claims as a natural right— the right to choose his tools, to decide when and how he will use them, and to participate in making the policies respecting the conditions of his work.

The teacher has not been allowed to help determine the criteria by which individuals are admitted to his profession, nor has he had anything to say about the nature of the training required for admission to the field of teaching. Even beauticians, plumbers, and carpenters have more control over the training and licensing of those admitted to their occupation than do teachers.[7] The unionization of teachers promises to move in the direction of greater participation in making policies and rules that govern the profession. But in the meantime, the impotence of the teacher in his own job and in his own profession often leads to intense dissatisfaction and in some cases ultimately to his departure from teaching.

The job of teaching also has been lacking in differentiation. About the only differentiation among teachers for a long time was based on the different levels of the educational system. Teaching in a high school carried more prestige and better pay than teaching in the junior high school, and teaching in the junior high was better than teaching in the elementary school. Fortunately, these distinctions have now been almost eliminated. While this is a momentous gain, the evils of the alternative are nearly as great. Lumping all teachers together and arranging them on a salary schedule in accordance with formal training and years of experience has depreciated the pride of workmanship. It has also led those who are more energetic and talented to make radical adjustments in their ambitions or to seek positions in other occupations that are open-ended in promotion and salary.

To sum up, explanations for leaving the field of teaching are mostly speculative, and, in particular cases, ad hoc. Nevertheless, it seems reasonable to suppose that a high proportion, probably 20 to 25 percent of those who complete preparatory programs each year, will continue to choose other vocations as long as their preparation lacks distinctiveness and thoroughness. A disconcerting number of teachers will continue to drop out after a brief experience as long as the profession has no share in determining the nature of the training and induction of those who become its members and no part in policy and decision making. As long as it makes no provision for recognition of merit and exceptional performance, and no provision for differentiation of functions within the job of teaching itself, there will be a tendency for experienced teachers to seek employment elsewhere.

Why Teachers Leave Deprived Areas

While the attrition of the teaching force in deprived communities can be attributed partly to the general exodus of teachers and partly to their mobility within the profession, much of it can be attributed to factors in the communities themselves. Working conditions and cultural advantages are always factors in the choice of where to work. Most physicians do not prefer to work in depressed rural areas or in the inner city. This is true of teachers as well. Teachers tend to move from the areas where salaries and working conditions are least attractive to communities where they are better and the chances of advancement more promising. Mobility tends to be from rural communities and the inner city to suburban areas. The rate at which teachers leave the depressed areas of Chicago is ten times greater than the rate of transfer in more advantaged communities.[8] In the borough of Manhattan, according to Haubrich, one-third of the teachers appointed to positions do not accept their assignments.[9] Many of those who do accept leave at the first opportunity. In a study of teacher attitudes in 15 major American cities it is reported that 17 percent of the teachers had been in their ghetto school for one year and 63 percent in their present position for five years or less.[10] The proportion of teachers remaining after five years dropped off radically. At the same time, some 88 percent of the teachers indicated that they were satisfied with their positions. But the rate of dropouts from the ghetto schools would seem to indicate that the teachers tend to move on even though they may express satisfaction with the school in general.

The teachers in the study just referred to were least satisfied with the working conditions, their teaching loads, and the community. About 63 percent were satisfied with their working conditions and approximately 62 percent with their teaching loads. But only 58 percent expressed satisfaction with the community, with 48 percent of these being only somewhat satisfied. A large proportion of the teachers were satisfied with their colleagues, supervisors, the pupils, and with their salaries and the flexibility permitted them in the classroom. These findings seem to indicate that the dissatisfaction of teachers in the ghettos stems from the community and the general conditions within the school itself. Since teachers seem not to prefer neighborhoods where working conditions are unfavorable, young and inexperienced teachers, who must accept positions wherever they find them, are often located in the disadvantaged areas. With the highest rate of turnover among beginning teachers, it is not surprising that schools in deprived communities suffer a high rate of attrition among their teachers.

One reason often cited for the reluctance to teach in disadvantaged schools is that the work there does not carry with it the same prestige as work in other communities. In fact, an appointment to the schools of disadvantaged areas often means to the teacher that his superiors have a low opinion of his ability. If so, that is a serious reflection upon the teacher training institutions. That teachers have this opinion is supported not only by the teachers themselves but by the well-known fact that teaching slow learners is felt to be much less desirable than teaching fast learners. This attitude is also a reflection upon the teacher training institutions and a sad commentary on the teaching profession. There is something basically wrong with teacher education when it produces teachers who look askance at difficult teaching situations.

Another reason teachers do not accept positions in disadvantaged areas, or hold them once they are there, is the feeling that they are not sufficiently trained to do the job. Some teachers become dropouts for the same reason that their students are dropouts: they quit because they fail. And they fail because they have not been trained to do the job before them. As Haubrich has so cogently pointed out, the teacher in the ghetto either rejects an appointment there or quits after a year or so because of "inability to comprehend, understand, and cope with multiple problems of language development, varying social norms, habits not accepted by the teacher, behavior which is not success-oriented, lack of student cooperation and achievement levels well below expectancies of teachers."[11]

It should be borne in mind, however, that the supplementary study of the National Advisory Commission on Civil Disorders shows that the entire sample of teachers studied were college graduates, and that 70 percent of them had received some professional training or had had some graduate study. Half of them had received some preparation for dealing with children in the deprived areas. These facts indicate that the deficiencies in preparation are not those which are associated with failure to meet requirements for the proper credentials. These are deficiencies which can be attributed to inadequacies in the training programs themselves.

There are apparently three main deficiencies in the training of teachers who are reluctant to teach in the disadvantaged areas and who drop out. First of all, teachers know almost nothing about the background of disadvantaged pupils and the communities where they live. All but a few have had little or no experience with other than middle class life until they walk into the ghetto schools or those of the rural slums. There they undergo cultural shock, an experience that disorients teachers because they are uprooted from their familiar surroundings. For example, studies show that teachers regard stealing, cheating, fighting, and other forms of extroversive behavior as most threatening to the classroom and themselves. Withdrawal forms of behavior, fearfulness, and hypersensitivity are thought to be less serious. Inner city children are on the average more outspoken and aggressive. Most programs of teacher preparation fail to equip the teacher with the skills and understanding necessary for dealing with conduct problems, especially aggressiveness. Naturally teachers are frightened and frustrated when they are confronted by behavior which they have never before witnessed and for which they are now made responsible.

Teachers fail because they have not been trained calmly to analyze new situations against a firm background of relevant theory. Typically, they base their interpretations of behavior on intuition and common sense. Teachers often appear to have no interest in children or even to fear them, because they simply lack the conceptual equipment to understand them. No matter how idealistic the teacher may be, he will soon find his hopes crushed if he is unable to understand and cope with disturbing pupil behavior. If the teacher is incapable of understanding classroom situations, the actions he takes will often increase his difficulties.

The teacher often harbors prejudices of which he may not be aware. His prejudices may be academic, as when a pupil is deprecated because he is slow to learn; or social class prejudices as, for example, when a teacher consistently . chooses the pupil with middle class manners for certain group responsibilities. There may be racial prejudices, as in the case of the teacher who expects less of a pupil because he is an Indian or a Negro. If a teacher is subtly or not so subtly prejudiced against pupils of a minority and expects little of them, he will get little from them. This is a special case of the venerable proposition that in the social sciences man creates the facts that make his hypotheses true. As Childs said many years ago,[12] if we believe that half of the people cannot think for themselves, and act accordingly, we will establish a society and a school system that will make it impossible for half of the people to think for themselves.

It is true that pupils cannot effectively shield themselves from the damaging attitudes and expectations of their teachers. It is also true that teachers who are inefficient in the skills of teaching and ignorant about the backgrounds of ghetto children often find they cannot explain or cope with their own attitudes. In this situation the insecurity of both the teacher and the student causes each to blame the other for the resulting chaos. The teacher then falls even further behind in his efforts to teach and the student continues to resist his instruction. Preparatory programs for teachers have ordinarily done little to sensitize the teacher to his own prejudices and to provide him with experience in the control of them.

A third area in which teachers lack sufficient preparation is in the skills needed to perform effectively in the classroom. The preparation of teachers today is barely a step removed from the apprentice system. In some cases, as in the MAT (Master of Arts in Teaching) programs, a pseudo-apprentice system has been set up. In any case, the teacher who is graduated from a teacher training program with a bachelor's degree is no more than an apprentice teacher. Much of his preparation has been irrelevant to the tasks he will face. And the student teaching program, at its best, fails to develop the skills of teaching. It is barely an introduction to the realities of the classroom and the school. Moreover, the work which the teacher may later do as a graduate student will also have little relation to the problems he will encounter in the school. It is now possible to design a program of teacher preparation that will contain a component of systematic training in the skills of teaching. There is no longer any reason for the beginning teacher to be left to work out his behavior patterns by trial and error.

Summary

Because of inertia, an individual tends to remain in his job rather than to move into something he knows very little about. This human trait probably accounts for a great deal of occupational persistence. Despite inertia, almost all individuals change jobs during their careers and a large number change occupations.

These are the changes we have attempted to account for. We have tried to explain the fact that persons leave the teaching profession in comparatively large numbers to go into other occupations or to pursue other activities. We have also attempted to account for the mobility of teachers within the profession itself from one community to another. In summary, it would seem that teachers in general will stay in the teaching profession if:

—they are adequately trained for the job they are expected to do,

—they are satisfied with the conditions under which they work,

—they are satisfied with the living conditions in the community where they work,

—they can make decisions about their occupational activities,

—the profession is self-respecting and has control over its own affairs,

—there are opportunities for advancement in their work, and

—financial incentives in the form of residential quarters, extended educational opportunities, travel, and other incentives are added to normal salaries.

There will always be some movement of teachers from school to school and from community to community. This is to be expected in any profession. But the retention of teachers in the ghettos and rural slums will be increased if the above conditions are satisfied. Whether a teacher decides to go into a disadvantaged community and remain there is not dependent upon the background and behavior of the children, upon their willingness to learn, or even upon their attitudes toward schooling and the teachers. Rather, it depends upon how well the teacher is trained, how much support the community gives him, upon the amount of control he has over his own working situation, and the prestige which his profession has earned in the community.

CHAPTER 3

MULTIPLE TEACHER ROLES
AND PREPARATION OF AIDES

Teachers are becoming more difficult to obtain at the very time the demand for teachers is increasing. Social service agencies are now understaffed and will probably remain so for the foreseeable future. The expansion of school enrollment and of services by other social agencies will put an increasing strain on sources of personnel. This means that these agencies are going to compete with one another for workers. The school, as one of these agencies, is in the competition; it can no longer get an adequate staff without drastic changes in the methods of recruiting and training teachers. The need for a new approach is emphasized by the fact that many teaching positions, especially those in rural communities and the inner city, are unattractive compared to positions in other fields.

Differentiated Teacher Roles

In the last few decades the teaching profession has followed a simple career pattern. A prospective teacher entered college, took the appropriate courses, completed student teaching, and became a certified teacher. Then, by taking more college work, he gained salary increases on a fixed schedule. Finally, with enough work and experience he might become a department head, supervisor, or principal. This career pattern is no longer entirely adequate. Today other means of entry into the profession and other modes of training need to be opened up.

Administration has long been differentiated into levels of responsibility and performance; subordinates were charged with the responsibility for directing various aspects of the educational program. The supervisory responsibility has likewise been divided into a number of roles reflecting the different levels of the educational program as well as the specializations within the program of instruction. But until recently the teacher's role remained intact. He performed every function from clerk to high-level performance as an instructor. However, the work of the teacher is now being differentiated into a number of roles. New sets of positions are being created ranging from pupil tutor to the executive or master teacher. Between these two, the positions being added call for varying degrees of preparation. Among these are teacher aides, technologists, assistant teachers, associate teachers, and well-established career teachers.

The historical precedent for the differentiation of the teacher's role is the monitorial system of the 1800's. A primary reason for the revival of interest in the division of instructional labor is the public demand that the school give personal attention to children rather than deal with them en masse. Individualized instruction and personal association of teacher and child, ideals long extolled by educational theorists, must now be made a reality. Nowhere is this demand more vociferously made than in the inner city where children are packed into schoolrooms and given very little individual attention. Close teacher-pupil relations are impossible without a great expansion of the instructional staff. There is not enough trained manpower for the schools to make individualized education possible.

No matter how diligent the school in its search for personnel, or how effective the preparatory program, the shortage of professional workers will remain. There is no shortage of raw manpower but a shortage of trained personnel. This can be relieved by breaking the teacher's work into sets of tasks that require varying degrees of understanding and different skills. These jobs can then be staffed by auxiliary personnel with ability but less than a college education.

Differentiation of the instructional staff is necessary to make the most efficient use of well-trained and effective teachers. The high-quality teacher must be given greater responsibility for planning programs of instruction and for directing the education of a larger unit of pupils than the ordinary classroom. However, his close relationships with individual pupils must never be broken by this extension of his responsibilities. To prevent this and to safeguard his other functions the master teacher must be supplied with an adequate staff of assistants who have varying levels of skill and understanding. In fact, the teacher aide, the beginning teacher, and the career teacher must be called upon to do much of the program planning in cooperation with the master teacher. Moreover, the problem of preparing a sufficient number of teachers can be solved only by differentiating the instructional staff and changing the modes of recruitment and training.

The Changing Career Pattern

Today there is a national movement to open up new careers to relieve unemployment and to provide opportunities for victims of poverty and racial discrimination.[1] The schools, being in great need of more effective programs and expanded services, are naturally a source of new jobs and new careers. With the passage of the Elementary and Secondary Education Act, the 1968 amendments to the Vocational Education Act, and the Education Professions Development Act, the movement to differentiate and expand the instructional staff was given extensive support. Even before these acts were passed, however, the concept of the teacher's role had been a major concern of the teaching profession, resulting in fundamental changes in its traditional form.[2] So, the combination of the national interest in new jobs and the search for a more effective use of the teacher strengthens the movement to create different levels of instructional personnel.

The differentiation of the teaching function means that an individual may enter the teaching field at a simple level. The most elementary level is that of pupil tutor. A pupil who is having difficulties in learning will often improve when taught by a fellow pupil. The child who is teaching increases his learning at the same time. This underscores the idea that the schools should provide opportunities for high school pupils to acquire teaching experience. The use of pupils to instruct each other might be as effective in inner city schools as others, because helping another person is a mark of prestige and a source of personal satisfaction. Both of these are often needed by youth of all backgrounds. Furthermore, instructional activities in art, music, drama, recreation, and the like can often be performed by high school pupils. While the involvement of pupils in tutorial activities cannot be accomplished wholesale, it can be employed widely enough to be valuable to the teacher and to give many young people a feeling of significance from having shared adult responsibilities. From these pupils the school could begin the recruitment of teacher aides, many of whom may ultimately become high-level personnel.

Another point of entry is the teacher aide. Young men and women who drop out of high school and have broadened their perspectives and increased their understanding may be enlisted as teacher assistants. There are also many high school graduates who could find themselves by working beside the teacher. In every community there are married women and unemployed men whose contribution to the education of children would be outstanding if they were given the opportunity. There is a vast reservoir of manpower from which to recruit subprofessionals for positions in the schools. The competition to employ these people will increase as other social services expand their personnel.

Thus, the point of entry into the field of teaching can be at the level of pupil tutor, teacher clerk, teacher aide, assistant teacher, or associate teacher, depending upon the individual's maturity, training, and experience. But no matter where the individual enters, the only restriction upon his advancement should be his aspiration and his willingness and capacity for work and study. Teaching should not be like some social service occupations where prior experience and training, even in related areas, count for nothing toward preparation for a higher position. No job in the field of teaching should be a dead end; no one need start all over again to advance.

Individuals who begin at any level should be encouraged to progress from one level to another if they have the capacity to learn. Of course, there will always be those who settle for jobs at lower levels, even though they might have advanced had they tried. But most will reach a level of responsibility compatible with their abilities and will function with the skill and understanding needed in their job.

According to one estimate, there are now over 100,000 teacher aides.[3] There are also assistant and associate teachers who are more directly involved in instructional activities. The number of these now employed in school systems is relatively small, but, with further differentiation of the instructional staff, the need for adequately trained personnel in these categories will rapidly increase.

The program of education outlined in the following chapters is based on the idea that the career track in education is being fundamentally altered. But most teacher educators still think in terms of the old path. What is to be done about theory courses, about subject matter preparation, student teaching, and field experience are questions entangled in a morass of graduation requirements, time allocations, and credits. Many of these questions will disappear when it is recognized that teacher education must be extended downward, begun for many before they finish high school, and extended into advanced professional and graduate work for those who have the interest and capacity.

The main consideration in the remainder of this chapter will be the training of teacher aides. The need for this type of personnel is most pressing in the rural and city slums. The overcrowding of classrooms in the inner city adds to the burden of the teacher and makes it practically impossible for him to give attention to the needs of individual pupils. A massive effort should be made to train aides to relieve teachers of much of the necessary detailed work that is not a part of instruction itself.

The Role of Teacher Aides

Teachers today assume responsibility for a large number of activities that have nothing directly to do with instruction. Once teachers are relieved of these obligations, teacher aides could take over to allow more time for the teacher to work more directly with the children.[4] For example, their work could include—

Tutorial activities:
—help children in their search for materials such as charts, pictures, and articles
—help children organize games and sports
—play with children and help them to use toys and playthings, and assist in supervising at recess
—assist teachers in the use of equipment such as projectors, viewers, and tape recorders
—help teachers with emotionally upset children by giving them personal attention
—serve as laboratory assistants
—help the teacher in reading and evaluating pupil work
—assist the teacher with children who have learning difficulties in reading and number work
—help the teacher with problem cases by working with the child outside of the class in activities he is interested in
—assist with instructional activities in art, music, on field trips.

Clerical activities:
—help the teacher with files of materials such as pictures, stories, and articles
—help with making and preparing materials of instruction, and type and duplicate instructional materials
—help teachers with examinations and records.

Housekeeping activities:
—keep order in cafeteria and hallways
—help in the library
—help in class with the distribution of materials
—supervise clean-up activities.

Despite the fact that the aide would have observed the performance of most of these activities when he was in school, he will not know how to do them, nor will he understand the school situations in which he will be working. The old saying that taking a watch apart is not the same as putting it together appears to hold here. Being instructed is not the same as instructing. No matter how mature an individual may be, or what his prior experience might have been, he will find the swift events of school and classroom a bewildering experience. It is therefore important that the initial training of a teacher aide orient him to the school system. It should also train him to do a few basic things so that he may gain a sense of immediate success. The first phase of preparation should emphasize clerical or housekeeping tasks rather than interpersonal relations with children. Nevertheless, he would be expected to observe pupils, interact with them in a variety of situations, and discuss his observations and experiences with the teacher.

The Training of the Teacher Aide

The history of teacher education is filled with accounts in which generation after generation of teacher educators stumble blindly, or sometimes with profound insight, toward the development of more effective programs. If there is anything to be learned from the experiences of the past it is that there is perhaps no one best way of preparing those who are to teach young people. It is not wise to be rigid. One should maintain a high degree of flexibility in both the agencies and programs of preparation. This lesson should be kept in mind as the profession develops plans for the training of auxiliary personnel. The program suggested here is no more than a working plan to be modified in the light of experience.

The training of the teacher aide would be carried on in the public schools in collaboration with a training center, a junior college, or a community college. Initial preparation would be provided in a week-long workshop. The staff of the workshop should be made up of teachers and supervisors from the public schools and members of a training complex or collaborating colleges. In addition to the basic tasks, the workshop would deal with the structure of the school, its rules and regulations, and the mores of the student group.

The transition from the initial period of training to the job should be gradual and the work load kept light. After the first week of training the aide would be employed on the job a half day each day for at least a month. In the part of the day he was not working, he could receive training for more clerical and housekeeping tasks. He would also receive help on the problems he encountered on the job. In short, he would spend a half day in school as a teacher aide and a half day in a training complex or college preparing himself for additional tasks, thus increasing his proficiency in the tasks he has already learned.

In the next phase of his training, the teacher aide would take on additional duties, working as much as four days a week. Under daily supervision by teachers, he would function as a member of a team of professionals and paraprofessionals. The remaining day would be devoted to study and training to develop his efficiency and expand his responsibilities. This phase would last approximately a year. During this time the teacher aide would acquire more clerical and housekeeping skills and additional skill in tutorial functions and interpersonal relations.

In this phase of training the teacher aide would be taking classes in a junior college or community college to supplement and enrich his work. Some of his study may be in subject matter fields, some in pedagogical subjects, or related fields such as anthropology and sociology. The training plan should involve him in studies that will contribute to his efficiency on the job. Since both his experience on the job and his studies in college would be designed to improve his proficiency, there is no reason why he should not be given college credit for his job experience as well as for his college work. In fact, a plan for allowing college credit for job experience should be worked out as an essential element in his program of preparation.

A second year of training would provide for more intensive work at the tutorial and interpersonal levels. The teacher aide would be working more and more with children, both individually and in small groups. He would also continue his college work. The question of whether he would take work in college beyond the second year of training as a teacher aide would depend upon his career plans.

Every organizational structure tends toward a rigid hierarchy in which the lower members of the echelon have restricted choices and are assigned activities which become routine. Adequate safeguards against this tendency emphatically need to be built into the instructional team as it develops. If this is not done the teacher aide will often find himself in a situation that stultifies his development. One of the ways of guarding against this is to sensitize teachers to the dangers inherent in the bureaucratic system and to make them aware of the importance of exploiting every possibility for broadening and deepening the experience of the teacher aide. But this will hardly be sufficient. In addition, those responsible for assignments and facilities should provide means for choice and discretion in the duties of teacher aides. On their side, the teacher aides within a school system or school district should be organized so they can air their grievances and suggest means to relieve them.

The training provided for the teacher aide is a form of apprenticeship. The aide takes college courses but his performance is developed by on-the-job practice and experience. For those who begin at this level and decide to pursue advanced training, it will be necessary to take further work at the college and university level, including a systematic program of training.

Recruitment of Aides

Teacher aides should be recruited from the community served by the school and other communities. They should be drawn from the ranks of those who have experienced social and economic deprivation and racial discrimination, as well as from the middle class. But the principle of integration should be scrupulously adhered to. It is important that the teacher aide not be oriented only to his own culture. For this reason, every school should be staffed with aides from a variety of backgrounds including all minority groups. The teacher aide who comes from the ranks of the poor would not only inject an important orientation into the instructional staff but also be a stimulus to other youth. They would see from his example not only that the future in general is not as hopeless as it appears, but that one can become a part of the educational system itself.

The number of teacher aides needed is so large that a massive recruitment program must be set in motion. This program should be designed with the clear understanding that the concept of teacher aides is still new to teachers, administrators, and members of boards of education throughout the country. The recruitment program must bring to their attention the advantages of employing teacher aides. Recruitment is a two-way affair. It needs enough people from whom to choose teacher aides, but school administrators and teachers must also want to utilize aides in the improvement of the instructional program.

The recruitment program might begin with an effort to inform school boards of the importance of teacher aides. In almost every state the school board associations are active and hold meetings to consider educational problems. It seems appropriate to enlist their leadership in the development of workshops and conferences to acquaint these employers and policy makers with the advantages of a differentiated instructional staff. This could be done by professional organizations in collaboration with state departments of education. The use of teacher aides in the schools is not likely to become extensive until boards of education throughout the country are aware of the importance of these aides to the efficiency of the school faculty.

Almost the same can be said about the faculties of common schools, junior colleges, and community colleges. Comparatively few teachers in the common schools understand the concept of staff differentiation and the various roles that subprofessional personnel could play.

Many teachers have no understanding of the sort of training that should be provided for the teacher aide. The idea of the conventional career pattern that dominates the thought of teachers needs to be radically reconstructed. It is necessary that the teachers who will be involved in the training and use of teacher aides understand fully that there are varying points at which individuals will be able to enter the teaching field.

State departments of education and the various organizations of school administrators, together with the leadership of junior and community colleges, should arrange for a series of workshops in each state so that teachers may come to understand the expanding functions of the instructional staff and the necessity for its differentiation. These workshops should give initial training to teachers in the use and procedures of training subprofessionals.

Through the agencies mentioned above, the work of teacher aides and the training of the teacher to use such aides can best be brought to the attention of the teachers in depressed rural areas, small villages, and suburban areas. For the inner city it would be more efficient to organize programs and workshops on a district-wide basis with the collaboration of community leaders, junior or community colleges, and local organizations of teachers and administrators.

Members of the lay community should also be involved in the recruitment of teacher aides. Their knowledge of available persons is often extensive enough to identify likely candidates and assess their potentialities for working with young people. Furthermore, the participation of members of the community helps to make the schools more of a reality in their lives and to give them a sense of involvement in the educative process. However, involvement of the community should not be sporadic and superficial. Explicit machinery must therefore be established for securing continuing community involvement. One example is a council whose members would be decided by open procedures that entail the broadest participation of citizens. Whatever machinery is established, it will be effective only if it taps the sources of community power sufficiently to hold officials accountable.

An informed, alert professional group working closely with the community is the best guarantee that teacher aides will be properly selected, trained, and utilized. A staff that is alive to its needs and is sensitive to the problems of social integration will be one that can find among its former pupils and the community those who would be most successful as teacher aides.

CHAPTER 4

THEORETICAL PREPARATION OF THE TEACHER

There should be several levels at which one can enter the teaching profession. One of these is the level of teacher aide as discussed in the previous chapter. Another is the beginning teacher. Beyond this level is the career teacher, master teacher, and various types of specialization such as teacher trainer and curriculum specialist. In this chapter we will begin to present a program for the beginning teacher. This program is more systematic and formal than that of the teacher aide. Here the teacher would be trained in the more sophisticated techniques and introduced to more advanced theoretical knowledge of teaching.

A prospective teacher may be admitted to this level without any prior experience as a teacher aide or any other experience in teaching. This level of preparation will be centered primarily in the college and university and will lead directly to a bachelor's degree and to an intern position in the school system. Of course, the teacher aide may also enter this level of training, and, as indicated in the previous chapter, should be permitted to count his experience and preparation as a teacher aide toward the bachelor's degree.

Preparation at this level should be prerequisite to programs leading to advanced degrees as well as initial training for the beginning teacher. Programs to prepare the teacher for differentiated roles and for higher levels of performance, as in the work of the master teacher, are discussed briefly in a later chapter.

Research and practical experience indicate that the program for the beginning teacher will consist of three basic interrelated parts: a theoretical component, a training component, and a teaching-field component. This and the next chapter will explore the first of these three constituents.

Theoretical Basis of Teaching

There are some who now assert that the job of teaching is little more than a craft, that it needs no theoretical basis. They claim that there have been many successful teachers who had no theoretical training. Still, although teaching has been carried on for a long time at the level of a craft (and some have done it skillfully), there is nothing in this fact to support the claim that teaching neither has a theoretical base nor needs one. Bridges and highways were built with a high degree of skill long before civil engineering was based on scientific knowledge. So it was in agriculture and medicine. The arts of man developed long before his theoretical knowledge.

The tasks that make up the job of teaching have been and are now being reconstructed and extended in the light of knowledge that has been gained from its underlying disciplines. Perhaps something should be said to make clear what is meant by theoretical knowledge. Such knowledge is abstract and may or may not have any reference to the real world. But in an empirical field, as distinguished from a symbolic one such as logic or mathematics, theoretical knowledge has some sort of reference to the manipulatory level of human experience. Theoretical knowledge makes up a large part of the content of the disciplines.

For present purposes, such knowledge may be said to consist of two forms. One of these is definitional. Definitions typically consist of categories into which objects and events are classified. They therefore express concepts. A second form is laws which usually take the form of conditional propositions. They are made up of two parts, a conditional and a consequential part. In other words, a set of conditions is stated, and a set of consequences associated with the conditions is also given in the same proposition.

Another kind of knowledge consists of particular propositions. In common language we refer to these as statements of fact. In addition there is knowledge which we refer to as practical. This form consists of statements of what is to be done if certain ends are to be achieved.

A few illustrations will help clarify these distinctions. The following are definitions from the discipline of psychology: (a) A response is a behavioral unit where the unit is characterized as a physiological event or as a meaningful act. (b) A reinforcer is a stimulus that increases the probability that a given response will recur. These two statements tell us how the terms "response" and "reinforcer" are to be used. The first one tells what sort of behavior will be called a response. The second one gives a category in which to place a given stimulus provided it increases the probability that a response will occur.

Theoretical knowledge, as we have just pointed out, also takes the form of conditional propositions. The following is an illustration: If reinforcers are withheld, a conditioned response already acquired will become extinct. This proposition relates one set of concepts (withholding and reinforcers) to another set of concepts (conditioned response and extinction). The empirical relation of these two sets of concepts is such that if the conditional part of the proposition occurs, the consequent will occur.

A statement of fact is a proposition about a particular observation. For example, John Draper's IQ is 125.

Practical knowledge more often than not takes the form of commands. Seat an angry pupil to reason with him. Tell a child whose work is good that he has done well.

The professional fields include these forms of knowledge and others that have to do with moral conduct and social norms because the professional worker must interpret objects and events, know the relationships among them, and know the means to attain particular ends. The professional worker must also know the facts about the objects and events with which he works. And since he serves social functions, the worker must be concerned with human values and social norms. By contrast, the disciplines are comprised mostly of definitions, conditional propositions, and factual statements.

It is important to recognize that the relation of theoretical knowledge to an occupation is typically indirect. The theoretical knowledge relevant to an occupation must be adapted to suit the particular reality that it meets. It is seldom possible, for example, to apply a proposition about learning directly to classroom conditions. There are more relevant variables in a classroom than in the experimental circumstances under which the proposition was established. It is just as important to know the pedagogical situation to which theoretical knowledge is to be applied as it is to know the knowledge itself. Only then can adaptations of such knowledge be made.

As long as there was very little theoretical knowledge to draw upon for the education of teachers, there was a fair degree of certainty that proper training of the teacher consisted of the mastery of the subject matter of his field of instruction and the development of teaching skills. But as theoretical knowledge has developed, the controversy over the education of the teacher has grown.

A few individuals, with little or no acquaintance with the growth of theoretical knowledge of pedagogy, wish to reduce teacher training to the development of teaching skills. There is also little agreement among those who train teachers on the amount of theoretical knowledge to be included in the program for beginning teachers. Some would weight the program with theoretical knowledge and would require considerable work in psychology, sociology, and philosophy. Others would limit theoretical knowledge to what can be shown to be directly related to the job of teaching, thus allowing little time to background knowledge.

Those who claim that theoretical knowledge is not essential to the development and use of the teacher's abilities are not aware of how this knowledge functions in practical situations. Since such knowledge seldom prescribes what to do in specific circumstances, these people claim that pedagogical theory is useless.

The Functions of Knowledge

Theoretical knowledge is used two ways in educational work: (a) to interpret and (b) to solve problems. Practical knowledge is used primarily to respond to familiar situations, that is, replicatively.[1]

The basic elements of theoretical knowledge are concepts. They are used to interpret what is observed. If one knows the characteristics and behavior of a phenomenon, he can identify it as a member of a class. But he still may not know how to deal with the phenomenon even though he has a sense of its nature, function, and worth. A physician uses concepts in diagnosing a disease, but he cannot derive a treatment from diagnostic concepts. If a treatment for a particular disease is already known, the diagnostic concepts enable him to decide whether the disease is one that can be cured by such treatment. But the concepts still function to interpret the conditions.

In a similar way, the teacher uses concepts to sort out the objects and events which he constantly faces. By putting them into familiar categories, he understands and organizes them in his experience. For example, the teacher is constantly observing the behavior of children. But he cannot understand a particular act unless he recognizes it as an instance of a type. A child answers a question. A teacher may decide that this bit of behavior belongs in a correct-answer category. He may then respond to it in an approving way. Or a child may respond to the teacher's question with a wisecrack. If so, the teacher may classify this behavior as attention-seeking. If one pupil attacks another, the teacher understands this act by considering it to be a sign of frustration. Terms such as "self-concept," "self-fulfilling," and "projection" designate concepts that teachers use to interpret behavior. But, as in the case of the physician, to interpret is not to treat. The teacher may understand behavior in terms of frustration and still have no better way of dealing with it than before he had this knowledge.

However, concepts can affect the teacher's attitude toward children. If a teacher interprets frustration as the source of a child's aggression, his attitude will not be the same as if he attributed the aggression to a defect in character, meanness, or simply to his being a "bad" person. The teacher thinks in terms of what he can do to change the situation. He looks for sources of frustration and ways to redirect the child's energy instead of demeaning the child.

One of the chief differences between a teacher who is theoretically-trained and one who is not is that the theoretically-trained teacher will perform with a set of sophisticated concepts taken from the underlying disciplines of pedagogy as well as from the pedagogical field itself. The teacher who is not theoretically-trained will interpret events and objects in terms of common sense concepts that have come from the experience of the race permeated with outmoded ideas about human behavior.

Besides interpreting what is observed, theoretical knowledge is applied in solving problems. When a new situation arises and established habits and skills are inadequate, a new procedure must be developed. For example, concepts have long been taught by citing instances. To teach a very young child the concept of chair, we may point to an object and say "chair" and later we may point to another object of the same kind and say "chair" again. By repeated citing of instances, the child gradually comes to think of a group of things called "chairs" and he will be able to identify other similar objects as chairs. There are several other ways of teaching concepts, most distilled from practical experience. Some of these have been tested to determine their effectiveness, but there remain many unanswered questions. One of these, recently studied, is: What is the effect of indicating similarities and differences among concepts that seem to be alike but are, in fact, very different? If the teacher compares and contrasts a concept unfamiliar to pupils with another similar one— for example, the concepts of imperialism and colonialism—the child becomes confused and the new concept is blurred. The explanation of this would seem to be that the cognitive strain becomes too great when a new idea is introduced in juxtaposition to one with which it may be confused. It would therefore seem better to compare and contrast after a new concept has been mastered, if the teacher desires to sharpen it by showing how it differs from concepts that may be mistaken for it.

To use knowledge in dealing with a problem such as this is different from using knowledge to interpret some object or event. Interpretation follows roughly the pattern of categorical subsumption. For example, a bit of behavior that is called frustration has such-and-such characteristics. The behavior which this child is exhibiting has those characteristics. It is therefore an instance of frustration. But the solving of a problem by contriving an original solution, although it may involve deduction, seldom can be reduced to categorical subsumption. A solution typically takes the form of an if-then proposition. Such propositions are made up of chains of concepts. Consider the proposition: If a concept (to be taught) is unfamiliar to pupils, introduce concepts with which it can be confused only *after* the new concept is learned. The conditional part of this statement contains the following concepts: pupil, unfamiliar, and concept. The consequent or "then" part contains the concepts: learned, new concept, confused, and after. The relations among concepts in an if-then proposition are such that they are expressible either as means-ends or as cause-effects relations.

Moreover, the solution is constructed not only from prior knowledge but from insights into new relationships. The applicative use is not just a matter of recalling knowledge but using it in contriving a solution. Effective application of knowledge in problem solving is not a simple undertaking. If it were, teachers would rely upon it much more often.

The teacher is seldom called upon to use theoretical knowledge to solve original problems. But once the solutions to such problems have been worked out and acquired by teachers, they will be used over and over again with appropriate modifications when teachers are confronted by similar situations. This is a replicative use of knowledge.

Many of the situations a teacher faces are similar to situations he has already met in his work. Furthermore, he has worked out ways of handling these situations or has learned ways in his training. He has built up a repertory of habits and skills and draws appropriate behavior from this supply with little reflection at all. A teacher reacts in much the following way: Tim has done well at last; it should help to compliment him immediately. Joe has made a mistake; he deserves to be shown how to correct the mistake. John is emotionally upset; he should be reassured by assigning him a task in which he can succeed. These are more or less automatic judgments that the teacher makes from moment to moment in the classroom. He skillfully repeats the performance that he has used on similar occasions.

Theoretical Content in a
Program of Teacher Education

Most of the controversy about the training of teachers is about the relative emphasis to be placed upon these three uses of theoretical knowledge. There are some who would reduce the training of teachers to the development of teaching skills used in a replicative sense. They would emphasize student teaching and so-called intern work and would eliminate formal courses except in the subject to be taught. There are others who would not eliminate formal courses in pedagogy, but would place primary emphasis upon student teaching and so-called internships at the undergraduate level.

Another group believes that even the undergraduate training of teachers should emphasize a large body of interpretive knowledge about teaching. It would insist that the attitudes of the teacher toward the children, school, parents, and the community are influenced by the concepts that the teacher brings to specific situations. These people insist that the teacher's attitudes are just as important as the habits and skills involved in teaching. They would put the interpretive use of knowledge equal to the value of student teaching and intern work.

Between these two positions is that of a third group which thinks of the teacher as a problem solver and insists that his training be one which gives him extensive experience in methods of dealing with problems as they arise in teaching. This group holds that the teacher is constantly faced with new situations. It would emphasize the uses of knowledge in problem solving and would design a teacher training program based on the habits and skills involved in research.

The view taken here is that the interpretive and replicative uses of knowledge should be given main consideration with little deliberate attention to its applicative use. The applicative use of knowledge is most significant to the highly trained teacher and the research worker. But teachers seldom use knowledge to work out solutions to novel problems. Like other workers, they try to take the easiest path and reduce their work to routine.

Although the teacher is faced by few problems that require original solutions, he is called upon constantly to diagnose situations and to make decisions. He may refer the more difficult cases to specialists, but, in most instances, he must deal with the situation himself. This calls for a high degree of theoretical understanding. The knowledge available for the interpretation of classroom behavior is greater and more powerful than the skeptics realize. It has accumulated from research in the behavioral sciences, philosophy, and pedagogy. The main problem of designing a program of teacher education is not the lack of theoretical knowledge, but how to select the knowledge and to train the teacher to use it.

The criterion for selecting the content of theoretical courses has most often been its relevance to the study of pedagogy rather than its relevance to the actual education of children and adults. Courses in pedagogy have been organized like liberal arts courses instead of the more practical organization in law and medicine where case study and clinical work are emphasized. As a result, the problems of education have been expanded beyond the ability of teachers to use pedagogical knowledge to advantage. Nowhere is this deficiency more apparent than in the schools' efforts to meet the needs of children who come from the poorer sections of the cities and rural areas. Study after study suggests that teachers do not empathize with children from very poor areas and with Negroes, Mexicans, Puerto Ricans, and Indians. Teachers depress the self-esteem and underrate the capacity of these children. They are unable to relate behavior at school to the home situation of the children, to understand the learning difficulties of the children, or to communicate effectively with their parents. Jonathan Kozol's book *Death at an Early Age* reports the tragic inadequacies of teachers of Negro children in the Boston public school system. He tells of middle-aged teachers giggling at the "primitive" feelings expressed at the funeral of a Negro child's mother. He tells of a teacher who called nine-year-old Negro boys "to the front, and, without questioning or qualification, she *told* them that they were lying and, furthermore, that she did not want contradictions from them because she *knew* them too well to be deceived."[2]

What should be the theoretical content of an introductory program of teacher education? To answer this is to identify concepts such as motivation, feedback, and explanation, which are needed to interpret situations the teacher most frequently encounters. No systematic analysis of the teacher's work has been made to determine the frequency of various types of teaching situations, but the most numerous are obvious from practical experience. Among these are situations in which the child is having difficulty learning and relating to the teacher, and situations in which judgments are to be made about the uses of instructional content. These and other situations provide the basis for selecting the theoretical knowledge.

An approach such as this requires a sharp break with the view that the inherent logic and integrity of courses in education should not be violated and that the student will profit mainly from systematically studying their content. This view relies heavily on transfer of learning, for it depends on the application of what is read or heard to the different real situations with which the teacher must deal. The focus of a teacher's theoretical study in a situational approach is not the content of a course but the situations he will meet and the tasks he will perform.

Systematic Courses

Not everything that the teacher needs to know can be learned from analysis of different types of situations, even though these situations can span the social spectrum. Just as it is important for the prospective teacher to learn concepts in the situation where they are to be used, so it is important for him to understand the theoretical context from which these concepts are taken. Nowhere is this fact more evident than in the development of cultural empathy. A teacher may understand from the analysis of a situation the conflicts that a child must have at home. But that is not the same as empathizing with the total social and cultural pattern within which the family and the child exist. It is one thing to be able to project one's self into a personal or family situation and it is quite another to understand, with a measure of comprehensive objectivity, the cultural conflicts that cause that situation. The teacher needs both of these forms of empathy. For this reason, the situational approach must be supplemented by a systematic study of pedagogically relevant aspects of the sociology, anthropology, and linguistics of the inner city, of rural poverty, suburbia, or any part of society from which a pupil comes. For this purpose, there should be systematic courses in educational anthropology, educational sociology, and social aspects of linguistics.

The situational approach should also be reinforced by a study of the relevant aspects of knowledge theory and the cognitive and affective processes of learning and feeling. The criteria and structure of knowledge and the concepts and laws of learning are so interrelated with one another, and with other basic considerations such as the teaching process, that a more complete understanding of them depends on a study of their extended intellectual context. There should be pedagogical courses dealing with different kinds of knowledge, such as analytic and contingent, prescriptive and evaluative, and singular and general. These elements would be analyzed and illustrated with examples from high school and college instructional materials. There should also be systematic courses in the cognitive and affective components of behavior.

It should be emphasized that none of this work ought to be confused with introductory courses in psychology or theories of knowledge. The purpose is not to lay the groundwork for further study in psychology or philosophy. Instead, it is to familiarize the teacher with the concepts he will be using in the training component of the program. The relevance of the content to be included in pedagogical courses in the social and linguistic aspects of education, in knowledge theory and psychology will depend on the analysis of the teaching situations. Therefore, the development of these courses must follow the development of the situationally-oriented part of the program. How this is to be done is the major task for the next chapter.

CHAPTER 5

THE SITUATIONAL TEACHING
OF THEORETICAL KNOWLEDGE

An effective teacher interprets, by means of theoretical knowledge, the events that happen in the classroom. A teacher's interpretation of what happens is important because he responds to the meaning of what he observes rather than to the happening itself. His interpretation of the situations that confront him is made in terms of his system of concepts, acquired in part from ordinary experience and in part from the technical and sophisticated systems of thought that make up the basic theoretical knowledge of pedagogy.

The question to be dealt with in this chapter is how to develop the teacher's conceptual system. Attempts have been made to answer this question by requiring formal courses in educational psychology and in the social and philosophical foundations of education. To acquire a set of concepts and to learn to use them in the interpretation of behavior is not an easy accomplishment. The theme of this chapter is that these concepts and their use can best be mastered, in the initial phases of teacher preparation, by studying actual behavioral situations and interpreting them with the concepts which are to be learned and subsequently used in teaching.

The first step in the formulation of a program for this purpose is to identify the most general categories of situations teachers face. Immediately we confront the fact that the role of the teacher includes more than teaching. The situations the teacher deals with are found not only in the classroom but also in the broader context of the school and community. As a first step, the following categories suggest themselves:

1. Classroom situations
   a. Instructional situations
   b. Situations of classroom management and control
2. Extraclassroom situations
   a. Situations that arise in planning school programs, working with peers and the administration
   b. Situations that occur in working with parents and other members of the community
   c. Situations that occur in working in professional organizations

The second step is to organize these situations according to the purposes of teacher preparation. Then the teacher should be instructed in the theoretical knowledge needed to understand them by examining and interpreting the situations.

Not all these situations or their interpretations will be discussed, for not every significant aspect of a teacher's preparation can be dealt with here, but we can consider a few classroom situations. The patterns of treatment suggested are also appropriate for extraclassroom situations.

Use of Behavioral Situations

Teaching behavior is complex, involving interactions with both pupils and materials of instruction. It cannot be studied in the classroom because behavior perishes as it happens and nothing is left to analyze except the memory or a check sheet. The fidelity of the memory is questionable and not detailed enough. The information contained on check sheets is almost no record at all. To learn to interpret situations they must be held *in situ* or reproduced at will approximately as they occurred. It is then possible to study situations at length and to use concepts (from psychology, philosophy, sociology, etc.) to interpret them. By being involved repeatedly in the process of analyzing and interpreting them, the prospective teacher will learn to interpret quickly and thoroughly the events and episodes that happen as he teaches.

Until the development of educational technology, it was difficult to reproduce teaching behavior. But today audio and video recordings of behavior can be made and studied in detail. They make it possible to teach theoretical knowledge of pedagogy in the context of its use as well as in formal courses.

To follow this mode of instruction it is necessary to have available an extensive supply of audio and video recordings of home, street, playground, and classroom situations, of committee meetings, and interviews. These recordings will be referred to here as protocol materials, behavioral situations, or simply as situations. Protocol materials should represent the most poverty-stricken and most affluent rural and urban communities, as well as all minority groups. They should also represent all grade levels and teaching procedures such as problem-solving, question-and-answer, and group discussion.

Unfortunately, the equipment and space necessary for adequate recordings are too expensive for most schools.[1] This cost may ultimately be reduced, but in the meantime the need for such materials is so urgent and so widespread that a central depository of video and audio recordings and kinescopes should be established and made available to training institutions at nominal cost. A number of institutions, federal and state agencies, and professional organizations could cooperate in the appointment and financing of committees to decide upon the kinds of recordings to be placed in the repository.

To teach theoretical knowledge of pedagogy in the context of its use, protocol materials should be classified and indexed for instructional purposes. These materials are now being used somewhat less effectively than possible because they are often used without proper analysis and without relation to objectives of instruction. An audio or video recording of a class period may contain all kinds of situations, such as explanation of an event or a teacher's response to a pupil's silly remark. To be used effectively, recordings must be analyzed and the situations contained in them identified and classified. Another condition for their effective use is that what is to be taught about the behavior in these situations must be decided before the beginning of instruction. This does not mean that additional viewpoints and insights will not emerge as a given situation is used in teaching. But these should occur in a context of purpose and understanding arrived at prior to the beginning of instruction. No instruction should begin until the instructor has studied the materials with extreme care.

The identification, analysis, and sequential arrangement of behavioral situations is perhaps the most difficult part of building a program of teacher education. This task should not be carried out haphazardly or left to the biases and fancies of a single instructor. There should be little, if any, curriculum-making on the spot in this phase of teacher preparation. Teaching behavior is an amorphous phenomenon that can be understood best by ordering and analyzing it into constituent operations. One of the most persistent mistakes in formulating programs for the preparation of teachers is the belief that anyone who looks at teaching behavior can tell what is going on and what is effective or ineffective about it. Much of the supervision of student teaching is permeated with this notion. The idea that teaching is simple and that anyone with a little talent who knows his subject matter can teach well is akin to this belief. Any serious effort to analyze teaching behavior and to arrive at dependable knowledge about it will quickly dispel such ideas.

Observation System as
Basic to Program Development

In order to build a program for instructing teachers-to-be in theoretical knowledge a faculty should become thoroughly familiar with the research on teaching behavior, especially the work on observation systems. Some of these are summarized in Gage's *Handbook of Research on Teaching*.[2] The literature on these systems is extensive. It is now being used with promising results as a source of hypotheses in experimental work. More to the point, however, these systems are replete with suggestions for breaking classroom interaction into behavioral situations. While the research on these systems is too extensive for review here, perhaps a brief discussion of their nature and how they may be used in developing a program for teaching theoretical knowledge of pedagogy is in order.

What any phenomenon is perceived to be is dependent upon a point of view. Concepts shape the viewpoint from which we observe a phenomenon and, in consequence, the facts we will note about it. So it is with teaching behavior. Persons with diverse conceptual orientations will identify disparate aspects of teaching behavior and will form quite different images of teaching as it goes on in the classroom. For example, Flanders[3] is oriented toward the affective elements that are involved in teaching behavior and his analysis reflects this view. In contrast, Bellack[4] begins his study of teaching with certain concepts about language and thinking and identifies cognitive elements in teaching behavior.

The fact that a description of teaching is influenced by one's conceptual system does not mean that one can observe in teaching whatever he wants to see. We can see in teaching only what is there, but teaching behavior is made up of many components, and, like any complex phenomenon, will yield diverse facts, depending upon the point of view from which it is observed.

Almost a score of observation schemes has been worked out in the last decade for the analysis of teaching behavior.[5] There are at least two emphases to be noted among these schemes. In the first place, some of the exchanges that go on between teacher and pupils can be looked at as the feeding of information into the learning process. The research of Bellack and other workers indicates clearly that this feeding operation is identifiable but that it is more complex than generally supposed. While this input process has to do with the control of the content of instruction, it also affects the relationship between teacher and pupil. Nevertheless, the feeding operation is primarily concerned with the development of effective ways of putting information into the learning process.

In the second place, teacher-pupil interactions can be observed in terms of the teacher's behavior toward the responses pupils make to the input process and to the teacher. Observations of teaching behavior which focus on these components emphasize emotion although the cognitive processes are implicitly engaged. The pioneering research of Withall on the social climate of the classroom illustrates this approach. Of course, any bit of teaching behavior may also be observed from both the affective and the cognitive standpoint.

Observation systems have made available a number of categories that can be used to identify behavioral situations and to select relevant theoretical knowledge. For example, if one were to follow the investigations of Bellack and his associates, one would classify situations as follows: structuring, soliciting and responding, reacting, selecting and directing teaching cycles. If one were to choose Flanders' analysis, the situations would fall into two main categories: those that call for direct behavior and those that require indirect behavior.[6] The question naturally arises as to which of the many observation systems should be used for the training of teachers. But a review of the research literature indicates that the analyses differ more in the labels used than in the substance of the categories themselves.[7] In other words, there is not as much variation among the analyses as the terminology seems to indicate.

Nevertheless, there remain important differences among observation systems even after differences in terminology have been reduced. So, the necessity of choosing among the systems, or else developing one eclectically, faces those who are responsible for designing a program of teacher preparation.

The choice would be simplified if the consequences of using any of these schemes had been worked out empirically. Any system of classifying teaching situations is best judged in terms of its fertility in answering significant questions about teaching and operating a school. The behaviors identified by the various observation systems have not been related empirically to measures of student achievement. In other words, we do not know whether the modes of behavior identified by one system are any more conducive to pupil learning than those of another system. Nevertheless, these systems tell us far more about the elements of teaching behavior and about the relationships among them than we have known before. They therefore open up for investigation a wide range of teaching behaviors that have been inaccessible.

Moreover, certain behaviors are performed by teachers as they carry on their work regardless of what they teach. The observation systems have made these explicit for the first time. To produce an alert teacher is to make him aware of the behaviors involved in teaching and to help him acquire a conceptual system for interpreting them. Furthermore, from analyzing protocol materials, he will be aware of the great variety of ways of handling each teaching task and of the different ways teaching behaviors and situations may be interpreted. This greater range of insights should render the prospective teacher more flexible, deliberative, and aware of a greater number of choices.

In the present state of knowledge about teaching behavior, a faculty bent upon revising its teacher training program will want to work out its own analysis of teaching behavior from a review of pertinent research literature. While a faculty will have its own orientations and traditions to satisfy, nevertheless it may find a few guidelines helpful for the development of a program for situational teaching.

Perhaps the first principle should be the ancient rule of beginning with the simple and moving to the complex. The initial analysis of protocol materials could perhaps begin with such simple categories as types of questions, demonstrations, and direct and indirect discourse. The advantage of beginning with these categories is that they make use of what the student already knows. But the content of these categories is soon exhausted and the concepts that can be taught by reference to them are limited. The next step should be to turn to more sophisticated analyses which involve the structure of teaching behavior, such as the categories suggested in the works of Biddle and Adams,[8] Smith and his associates,[9] and Bellack.[10] A third guideline is that the categories of analysis should represent an appropriate balance among affective, cognitive, social, and psychomotor aspects of teaching.

Theoretical Knowledge in Interpreting a Teaching Situation

Let us turn now to a few illustrations of how the general category of classroom situations, referred to earlier, may be broken into subcategories for program development. From research on observation systems we know that teachers become involved in situations where the following are being taught: values, causes, reasons, concepts, interpretations, rules, procedures, and particulars. For illustration we shall use a spate of discourse from a high school biology class. The group has been discussing the nervous system and at this point it is considering the parts of the central nervous system and their functions.

Teacher: What is the midbrain?
Pupil: The smallest portion of the human brain?
Teacher: All right. It's the smallest part, but where's it located?
Pupil: Just above the pons and the cerebellum?
Teacher: Yes. As we move up, we would find under here a pons— these crossed nerve fibers—and then on up above that, we will find a midbrain, which is made of what kind of material?
Pupil: Nerve fibers?

Teacher: Nerve fibers. And what would be its function?

Pupil: It, I imagine, would carry messages from the cerebral hemisphere and from the pons and stuff? The pons.

Teacher: All right, it will also be a pathway or a conductor for impulses. We would also find that it will be a sort of connecting link or a binding tissue for the cerebrum with the cerebellum, or just below the cerebellum.

This set of verbal exchanges between teacher and pupils appears to be simple, and, in some quarters, would be dismissed as a mere question-answer procedure. But is it as simple as all that? If this protocol material were used to teach theoretical knowledge, the analysis would raise a number of questions—among them, the following: (a) What is the objective of the discourse? Is it to teach a value, a cause, a concept, an interpretation, or what? (b) What kinds of information are fed into the learning process? (c) How is the information mediated? (d) Does the teacher use reinforcers? If so, what are they?

From a discussion of these questions in this situation, and in others like it, the prospective teacher would be expected to learn (a) to identify a situation in which a concept is being taught, (b) to recognize a concept and to analyze it, (c) to recognize the sorts of information used to teach concepts, (d) to be aware of the sorts of verbal acts used in teaching concepts, and (e) to recognize reinforcers.

From a study of behavioral situations in which concepts are being taught, it is possible to identify the following modes of input:
A teacher:

—cites one or more characteristics of the referent class,

—cites a set of characteristics sufficient to identify something as an instance of the class,

—cites a class of which the referent is a subclass,

—describes a referent as a subclass of a given class,

—compares the referent to something else,

—tells what the referent is not,

—tells the opposite of the referent,

—tells the difference between the referent and something else,

—notes the similarities or differences between two or more instances of the referent class,

—cites an instance of the referent,

—cites something that is not an instance of the referent class,

—tells how an instance may be produced, or

—gives evidence that a suggested instance is in fact an instance.[11]

A person who is prepared to teach understands the structure of concepts as well as these input operations. Yet most teachers are not aware that they perform them. They often perform these operations poorly because they have neither been taught to think in this way about teaching concepts nor trained in the appropriate skills.

Regardless of social class or racial origins, all children perform these same operations but in varying degrees of complexity. Children do not differ from one another because some have concepts and some do not, nor because some build concepts one way and some another. Children have differing degrees of concepts, often rich and varied, regardless of their backgrounds, rural or urban, rich or poor. Often the same concept may be expressed in very different words; for example, some children use the word "cop out," though the teacher would use "quit." Sometimes prejudices are manifested in the teacher's response to an expression; for example, a white child may say "cop out" and get an understanding response different from what the black child gets, not because of what is said but because of who said it. As a teacher is taught through analyzing instructional situations, he comes to understand the different modes of expression that are used by children of different backgrounds. The situational approach is valuable because it enables the teacher to come very close to reality. But being close to reality is insufficient. It is interpretation of reality that is important in teacher education.

An analysis of protocol materials of classroom activities shows that a teacher is involved not only in the teaching of concepts but of values, procedures, causes, reasons, rules, facts, and skills, and that each of these requires its own kinds of information and input operations. It goes without saying that input behavior can be analyzed in different ways, depending on the purpose. The examples above are given, not to indicate what the analysis should be, but to point out that theoretical knowledge can be taught at sophisticated levels of analysis as well as in different kinds of situations. A study of situations and the operations involved in them expands the teacher's usable theoretical knowledge more than does the study of the verbal framework of a textbook.

Theoretical Knowledge in Analyzing Errors

The teacher also makes diagnoses. As the pupil interacts with the teacher and other pupils, he may claim something to be a fact when it is not. Then the teacher in one way or another makes the student aware of his error. Perhaps he will alter his input operations to help the pupil see what the state of affairs actually is. The task of helping pupils with factual errors is ordinarily performed by teachers without difficulty.

Errors in conceptualization or causal relations and evaluations are somewhat more complex. If a pupil says that a particular act of a government is an expression of nationalism, when it is not nationalism at all, the teacher knows that the error is a mistaken use of this concept, but he may not know the source of the error. The error may be caused by incorrect factual information. It may be due to an erroneous criterion which leads the pupil to include the act in the category of nationalism. Or it may be due to the fact that the pupil is confusing the concept of nationalism with another concept, such as imperialism or colonialism. To determine which of these errors is exemplified by the pupil's mistake requires a great deal of understanding of the structure of concepts as well as of the concept itself and others easily confused with it.

The same sort of analysis can be made for errors of generalization where cause-effect relationships are involved. Such errors will range from overgeneralization to the misunderstanding of relationships among variables. The theoretical training of a teacher requires much experience in identifying and analyzing the source of pupils' mistakes in situations where causes, values, procedures, and the like are being dealt with.

Interpreting Interpersonal Relationships

The protocol materials should also reflect the effect of the teacher's behavior on the child's personality. The child not only responds to the teacher, but the teacher is constantly responding to the child. In these responses the teacher may be building the self-esteem of the child or he may be acting in a way that deteriorates the child's ideals and motives.

The effect of a teacher's behavior, in most respects, is the same on affluent children as it is on poor children. It is important to realize, however, that the verbal and nonverbal modes of ingratiation and insult of the middle class will vary in some degree from those of the lower socioeconomic class and that the variations are accentuated by social origins as well as other circumstances. The self-concept of any child has a social reference. He accepts himself in relation to how others respond toward him. A teacher who pays no attention to a child's work when the child is aware of the fact that he has not done his best may in effect be telling the child that he is not significant. In a program of theoretical training it is valuable for the teacher to have extended experience in analyzing protocol materials where the response of teachers to the behavior of pupils is exemplified.

In the analysis, the prospective teacher will see a considerable number of ways of approving a child's behavior. He will see that the teacher may:

—*emphasize,* repeat with falling inflection, agree with the child, indicate correctness without evaluation, give a nod of acceptance in a matter-of-fact way, agree to examine the problem of the pupil, write the child's response on the board, elicit confirmation of his, the teacher's, understanding of a child's statement (without skepticism) ;

—*evaluate responses* or performance of the child or class in a positive way, make a judgment of value or of the quality of behavior, praise or express liking or gratitude for action or response of child or class;

—*redefine plus* elaborate an idea suggested by a child, release a child from normal expectations, cite extenuating circumstances, tentatively accept a suggestion with a qualifying phrase;

—*give verbal or nonverbal support,* encouragement, show appreciation verbally or nonverbally, express confidence, enjoyment, show affection with expression, gesture, or physical contact, give assistance in finding something in a book (not instructing or demonstrating) ;

—*take role of equality with child,* become a co-participant, use expressions of common courtesy, become a member of a group in putting on a skit, follow suggestions of a child, tell jokes, make a play on words for enjoyment of the class;

—*express sympathy with child,* give reassurance, show understanding, give a pat on the back, smile at a child having trouble, show concern for problems, comfort;

—*elicit group attention,* call attention to an approved behavior, hold up a product of a child or group for all to see;

—*offer or give special privileges,* tangible gifts, superior mark or grade;

—*show personal interest in child's concerns,* comment on the interest, experience, or perceptions of a child or of a class.[12]

The teacher-to-be will see also that among disapproving behaviors are the following, many of which, depending on circumstances, may be injurious to the child's self-concept:

—*physical disapproval,* shaking, slapping, ear-pulling, spanking;

—*physical restraint,* isolation, exclusion, banishment, sending child to the office, removing the child's desk to the corner of the room;

—*negative evaluation,* direct contradiction of the opinion of the child, qualifying a child's response negatively, assigning a low grade, defining the response of the child in a negative way;

—*social shaming,* belittling, ridiculing, using sarcasm, public castigation, singling out a child and berating him.[13]

Responding to the behavior of a child is far more complex than the description above indicates. To be helpful, the teacher must take into account the correct timing of his own behavior and must make clear which part of the pupil's behavior he is approving or disapproving. Also, the modes of approving and disapproving will have different nuances depending upon the cultural origins of the child.

Conduct Situations
and Theoretical Knowledge

The teacher's education should include an analysis of conduct situations. It is generally held that in a healthy classroom atmosphere a teacher will have no need for special techniques because few problems of misconduct will arise. Of course a classroom in which the social atmosphere is conducive to learning and proper conduct will have a minimum of disruptive behavior, but even under the best conditions the teacher will encounter misconduct. A teacher cannot have control over all the factors which influence the behavior of a child at any one time; therefore, problems of personal relations will arise no matter how good the classroom atmosphere may be.

There are too many acts of disruptive behavior to be described and interpreted individually. These acts should be classified into groups of those which can be explained and handled in similar ways. Training programs are often ineffective because no such grouping has been made. Programs up to now have used formulas taken from practical experience and have used them without reference to the origin of misconduct. The protocol materials used to develop the understanding of conduct must be classified. Acts of misbehavior have been grouped by factor analysis into five categories. They are presented here to illustrate what may be developed for the purpose of grouping situations for instruction:

—*physical aggression:* fighting, hitting, ridiculing or making fun of others, pushing others, bossing, bullying, and scuffling
—*peer affinity:* affected gestures, paying attention to another pupil instead of the work at hand, moving without permission, and wandering around
—*attention seeking:* seizing or hiding property of others, making unnecessary noise, making wisecracks, asking silly questions, and making silly remarks
—*challenge of authority:* talking aloud, creating a disturbance, protesting amount or conditions of work or teacher's request, and refusing to obey authority
—*critical dissension:* making criticism or complaint that is unjust or unconstructive, laughing so as to disturb others, making strange noises, whistling, shouting, throwing objects, playing with objects[14]

While these categories represent roughly the types of misconduct which the teacher will encounter, they do not indicate how he is to react to them. In the situational materials, however, the teacher in training can see how children have responded. In some cases it will be possible to hypothesize ways to handle various types of situations. Nevertheless, the theoretical instruction of a teacher should explain these different types of conduct.

The theoretical preparation of the teacher should, all in all, reconstruct the teachers' attitudes so that they come to see the children, regardless of social origin, as having extended potential. To help bring this about, the teacher educator must have a rich supply of realistic descriptions and reproductions of actual situations as instructional material.

Extraclassroom Situations

Although situations outside the classroom are an important component of a program of teacher education, they will be given cursory treatment in this essay. The following are a few of the teacher's activities to be considered in the preparation of protocol materials. Teachers participate in one way or another in:

—*collective activities:* salary committees, grievance committees, general meetings, academic freedom committees, etc.

—*staffing activities:* guidance teams, problem cases, etc.

—*program activities:* curriculum committees, departmental meetings, conferences with principal and supervisors, etc.

—*community activities:* parent conferences, participating in community groups such as parent-teacher meetings, etc.

Extraclassroom situations, when identified and analyzed, help define the role of the teacher in the school and community. While they are only indirectly related to the teacher's classroom work, an understanding of these situations, and adequate performance in them, may fundamentally affect the classroom itself.

Content and Mode of Instruction

When the protocol materials have been collected, classified, and analyzed, how are they to be used? They are the objects, not the means, of study. In themselves they contain little theoretical or pedagogical knowledge. They are samples of behavior to be examined. But with what cognitive resources are they to be studied? This question brings us to the problem of what the content is in teacher education and where it is to come from.

To understand either the input or diagnostic phase of teaching is to understand the nature of knowledge and its logical structure. To the extent that a teacher does not understand the nature of concepts, causes, and values, he does not fully know the subject matter of instruction, and he lacks the logical, psychological, and linguistic sophistication that enables him to manipulate content to the advantage of the pupil. Without this knowledge he can only superficially identify a pupil's deficiencies in comprehension. An examination of the input operations shows that they are rooted in philosophy as well as in the psychology of learning. Part of the content of a training program is found in works on types of knowledge and their logical and semantic character.

Knowledge relating to input and diagnosis must also be taken from the field of psychology. A few results of research will clarify the point. There is evidence that the introduction of another concept when a pupil is learning a similar one might cause confusion and reduce the effectiveness of instruction. This situation can be easily shown on videotape so the trainee will be able to see in reality the effect of this confusion on the learner. It is known that one's perception shapes his response and what he will learn. If the pupil's response is different from what is expected, the teacher should explore the pupil's view of the situation. The teacher will often find that the perceptions of children from poverty-stricken backgrounds are quite different from his own. For instance, a child whose life is filled with conflict may think of a labor strike in a very different way from the teacher. In protocol materials where conflict situations are shown, much of the psychological knowledge about perception and attitudes can be learned meaningfully.

Various ways teachers respond to the pupils are explained by reference to psychological concepts. These principles are not understood simply by reading the results of psychological studies. Concepts like self-image, self-fulfillment, differential reinforcement, and vicarious reinforcement should be shown in protocols and analyzed in context. The same is true for explanations and treatments of deviant behavior, as well as other results of research. Apart from situational instruction, theoretical knowledge is apt to remain pedagogically useless.

Protocol materials should not be used merely to illustrate points in education courses. The whole procedure should be turned about so that the principles of the psychological, sociological, and philosophical studies, as well as those of pedagogy, are brought to the analysis of protocol materials, not the other way around. These materials suggest the knowledge that is relevant to the teacher's work.

The study of protocol materials will not only result in the prospective teacher's ability to understand and to interpret situations he will face in the classroom, school, and community; it will also increase the teacher's interest in theory, for he will see clearly for the first time that it is useful.

The theoretical program may take various shapes, depending upon the institution. It may consist of informal seminars, clinics, or theory centers. The kind of organization is not as important as emphasis on the interpretive use of knowledge and the development of concepts to explain the behavior seen in protocol materials. It is important, however, that the work be orderly. There is no place for predominantly opportunistic instruction or haphazard study in the theoretical preparation of teachers. When protocol materials are categorized into types of situations, the types can be arranged in a meaningful order which will become the basic structure of the theoretical program. The idea that all theoretical training of the teacher can be given on the spot is erroneous. It would strip teacher education of its theoretical content and reduce the teacher to a superficial technician. If teacher education for all schools and all children is to become more effective and realistic, it must include a heavy emphasis upon the theoretical. This theoretical content must be taught and learned in the context of systematically ordered protocol materials and simulated situations and developed more fully in systematic courses.

Form of the Program
in Pedagogical Theory

The form of the program may take different shapes at different institutions, but on the whole it will consist of courses which emphasize the interpretive use of knowledge. Their purpose will be to explain the type of behavior represented in the protocols.

Two courses would be required at the initial level of college preparation.

Course A. Teaching Behavior. The emphasis in this course would be upon analyzing and interpreting the various types of instructional situations, including tasks of classroom management and control. Protocol materials would be the basis of the course. The outcomes of the course should be as follows: grasp of the relevant concepts and principles; ability to interpret teaching-learning behavior; sensitivity to the behavior of pupils and to their psychological states; better grasp of the character and structure of different types of knowledge; understanding of how the subject matter of instruction is manipulated in teaching; and understanding of behavior involved in diagnosing and responding to pupils' responses. The content would be taken primarily from logic, semantics, knowledge theory, and psychology, as well as from pedagogical sources.

Course B. Nonclassroom Teacher Behavior. The materials in this course would be protocol also. They would be representative of the situations found in committee meetings, staffing conferences, parent conferences, and meetings with defiant members of the community. Again the instruction would be interpretive and the relevant content would be found in the literature on guidance and counseling, social psychology, sociology of education, social philosophy, collective negotiations for teachers, and other pedagogical sources.

Procedure of Program Development

By way of summary, perhaps a word or two should be said about the procedure of program development implicit in this chapter. The procedure consists essentially of the following phases:

—*Collect* audio and video materials of the work of teachers.
—*Review* research on teaching, and review such other research as may be relevant, and formulate categories of the situations encountered by teachers.

—*Analyze, classify, and index* the audio and video materials into the situational categories that have been formulated.

—*Select* concepts, generalizations, and facts relevant to the comprehension of the situations from appropriate sources.

—*Arrange* the protocol or situational materials into courses of instruction.

—*Analyze* protocol materials to make sure they are fundamentally understood for instructional purposes.

—*Try out* protocol materials on a small scale with a few teachers in training.

—*Make revisions* that the tryouts indicate.

—*Put the program into operation* for the total student body in training.

—*Make revisions in the program* that wider experience and evaluation indicate from time to time.

These procedural steps formalize what has to be done to develop a program for the initial preparation of the teacher in the theoretical knowledge essential to his success. This knowledge is useful because it enables the teacher to tell the various meanings of pupil behavior as well as the behavior of others with whom he interacts. But to understand behavior is not the same as knowing how to respond to it. To respond properly requires a multiplicity of skills that can be acquired most effectively in a program of training. In the next three chapters we shall consider the nature of such a training program.

CHAPTER 6

AN APPROACH TO SYSTEMATIC TRAINING

Colleges and universities have begun to realize that they have been preparing people to teach only in middle class schools. As educators have become aware of this, they have made several changes in teacher education programs to prepare teachers better.

Current Programs

The changes in conventional programs have been influenced by a few familiar ideas. The most influential idea is that field experience is necessary to acquaint the teacher with the background of his pupils, advantaged, disadvantaged, or otherwise. Part of a teacher's preparation is to familiarize him with the community agencies and the street and home life of inner-city or rural neighborhoods.

Some programs provide the prospective teacher with an orientation to the disadvantaged pupils and neighborhoods by a series of firsthand experiences through community agencies serving disadvantaged youths. These contacts are usually supplemented by seminars in which the issues and problems of youth are explored. Resource personnel may include social workers, settlement house employees, and others serving disadvantaged youths.

Prospective teachers are also brought into contact with disadvantaged youths in both classroom and neighborhood settings. For instance, the prospective teacher may work as a tutor prior to student teaching or apprenticeship. These programs also provide opportunities for students to study their experiences in weekly seminars. The major advantage of these direct experience programs is that they make the prospective teacher face reality.

Some staffing and program changes support prospective teachers as they are placed in disadvantaged areas. This is done mainly through the utilization of outside personnel, usually public school teachers and supervisors, who either supervise the trainee or teach him in more formal situations and who are chosen for their success in school or community programs for disadvantaged youths. These and other forms of participation probably also strengthen the partnership between public schools and colleges in the preparation of teachers.

At the heart of these developments is the idea that new knowledge about the disadvantaged should be supplemented by actual experience with them. This assumption follows a time-honored concept in teacher education that practice in actual situations should supplement the studies one pursues at college. The practical difficulties of implementing this in the colleges throughout the country explain the relative slowness with which so-called apprenticeship programs have developed, especially in disadvantaged areas.

Another recent development is the Teacher Corps. Drawing on a variety of educational ventures and utilizing the drive and enthusiasm of young people, the Teacher Corps draws its candidates from college graduates who have had little or no formal preparation in teaching. It puts the corpsman through a two-year program which, again, places heavy emphasis on experience with the disadvantaged. In some cases, the experiential aspect of the program has been turned about. Negro corpsmen from the ghetto have been placed in middle class communities, as in the Bethel project.[1] A subsidiary feature of the program is the cooperation which is required between public schools and colleges, even though there has been a low commitment to the program by the colleges. While the assurance of a paid apprenticeship which is an integral part of the Teacher Corps may be a major inducement, it is clear that the Teacher Corps is utilizing some of the talent and energy which today's young people can direct to the education of disadvantaged youths.

In addition to field experience, the results of research in family structure, language of minority groups, and research in the culture of poverty are being used in courses, seminars, and workshops to familiarize teachers with the culture of their pupils. This type of instruction is about all that some programs provide to prepare teachers to understand the cultural backgrounds of their pupils, regardless of their social origins.

All of these ventures are commendable in some respects. They give the prospective teacher firsthand experience that should perhaps prepare him better than the abstract courses and formal examinations of the conventional teacher education program. But putting the prospective teacher out in the "streets" may only reinforce a cult of uniqueness because he is too often prepared to see the differences rather than the similarities. Then, too, the motivation for exposing the trainee to the deprived community is often to get him used to the members of the community so he won't be shocked by their "strange" customs, rather than to develop his ability to interpret objectively the situations and circumstances he observes. It is necessary to remember that mere proximity does not always result in useful knowledge. It may be detrimental if the trainee is not prepared conceptually and emotionally for the experience. Put an untrained person who is weighted down with fear, distrust, and dislike of automobiles behind the wheel and he may become convinced that he cannot, should not, and does not want to learn to drive.

The Teacher Corps and all other programs that would prepare teachers primarily through direct experience suffer from one crucial defect. They provide for very little training; they put all their trust in field experience, community work, and so-called apprentice activities.

Teaching is a complex activity, although to the uninformed it appears so simple that anyone can do it. Its complexity lies in its different types of techniques: material, social, intellectual, and emotional. Few, if any, other occupations involve all of these. The teacher handles materials such as books, projectors, and other instructional products; these require skill in thing-techniques. The teacher also relates to a large number of people: pupils, colleagues, laymen, in highly significant ways and often at crucial points in their lives. To handle these relationships skillfully one must be a master of techniques of social interaction and of empathizing. The teacher is involved in the manipulation of ideas as they relate to the growth of the pupil. He can be successful at this only if he is, in fact, skilled in linguistic, logical, and psychological techniques.

To acquire skill in these techniques taxes the capacity of the most talented individual. Very few people pick up more than a small repertory of them; the average person must work for years to acquire a few of these techniques. Even then he must often rely on bits and pieces he has picked up. It is generally believed that student teaching and field experiences are the most effective ways of acquiring these skills. For current programs this assessment is perhaps correct. But the belief that direct experiences, studied and analyzed in seminars and supplemented by apprentice teaching, even under the best of supervisors, is the best way to produce the skills needed in the modern school testifies to the intellectual inertia of those of us who work in the field of teacher education. Today new things are possible.

Almost all teachers are now prepared in programs that provide little or no training in teaching skills. These programs consist of courses in the sociology and philosophy of education, learning theory and human development, and in information about teaching and

70

management of the classroom. These are taught apart from the
realities that the teacher will meet and are considered preparatory
to student teaching. While student teaching usually comes after the
formal courses, it frequently has little relationship to them, and is
ordinarily inadequate preparation for the responsibilities given the
beginning teacher. The trainee studies theories that lead nowhere,
then does his teaching with little theoretical understanding of the
situations he meets.

More recent programs, for example, the MAT (Master of Arts in
Teaching)-type programs, differ little from conventional ones, except
in their disregard for theory. They reduce theoretical work to almost
nothing and place great emphasis upon learning on the job. Concepts and principles are discussed in seminars, along with the
trainee's problems and observations. These programs suffer from
lack of thoroughness and from inadequate diagnostic and remedial
techniques of training. The behavior of the student teacher in a classroom situation cannot be described except from the student's memory
or the supervisor's notes. This type of information is notoriously
inadequate. The fact that the trainee's memory and the supervisor's
record often do not coincide threatens their rapport. Inadequate
information and conflicting views on what happened are not conducive to learning. Furthermore, these more recent programs incorporate the worst features of opportunistic instruction. The supervisor
of the student teacher typically works without a systematic conceptual framework to help him analyze and guide the trainee's
performance.

The belief that either of these programs provides for training rests
on the gratuitous assumption that firsthand experience and student
teaching are training. At best, student teaching is a reality from
which the trainee learns by trial and error and a minimum of feedback. The situations that arise in his teaching are fleeting in tenure
and can be discussed only in retrospect. He cannot "work through"
the situations again to correct his behavior because classroom work
moves rapidly from situation to situation and no situation can be
reinstated for the practice of a technique.

The absence of a training component in teacher education is perhaps its principal defect. This component has not been devised
because theoretical courses combined with student teaching have been
considered adequate in principle and because the essentials of training have not been explicitly thought through.

A Concept of Training

The college training of a teacher should take cognizance of two
assumptions: first, the type of community in which he is to teach
is not definitely known; and, second, training beyond the beginning

level will be relied upon to provide him with skills that any specialized role will require. Minimal abilities which a program of teacher education should develop are the ability to:

1. perform stimulant operations (question, structure, probe)
2. manipulate the different kinds of knowledge
3. perform reinforcement operations
4. negotiate interpersonal relations
5. diagnose student needs and learning difficulties
6. communicate and empathize with students, parents, and others
7. perform in and with small and large groups
8. utilize technological equipment
9. evaluate student achievement
10. judge appropriateness of instructional materials

Each of these may be exhibited in a number of ways; for example, a number of reinforcement techniques were listed in the preceding chapter. A consideration of all of the abilities will disclose that each can be expressed in many different behaviors.

The understanding of these abilities, as noted earlier, is to be developed in the theoretical component of the program. But skill in the performance of these abilities should be developed in the training component. The focus of study in a training program is the trainee's own behavior, not the content of courses or some model of performance. This is in sharp contrast with the theoretical component where it is the situation that is to be examined and understood. In training, it is the trainee's performance that will be observed, analyzed, and modified.

To train someone is to guide him to acquire a certain skill. The trainee is put in a situation where he can perform the skill, then is stimulated to perform it. His performance is analyzed and assessed. He and the trainer suggest changes in his performance. The more acceptable performance is supported through reinforcement by the trainer. Reduced to its formal structure, the training process must include the following elements:

—establishment of the practice situation
—specification of the behavior
—performance of the specified behavior
—feedback of information about the performance
—modification of the performance in the light of the feedback
—performance - feedback - correction - practice schedule continued until desirable skillfulness is achieved

In order to train new teachers and to continue the training of those in service, it is necessary to design a program and sets of training materials that will incorporate each of the above elements.

Training Situations

Training always takes place in specially designed situations. The two main kinds of training situations are real and simulated. Real situations are used where it is possible to repeat the basic elements of a situation without resorting to role playing. Almost all instructional situations can be of this type. For example, the trainee can be told to teach spelling words to five or six assembled children. All the elements in this situation are genuine. No part of it has to be acted out. Situations are simulated when a real situation is not possible. It is impossible, for example, to have a discipline problem arise at will. This must be set up artificially.

Either of these two types of situations occurs in two forms: one in which the performance of the trainee is specified, and one in which the performance is suggested but not specified. The difference between specified and unspecified forms is the degree to which the trainee's behavior is prescribed. In the specified form, the technique is prescribed as exactly as possible. In unspecified situations, the technique is left to the trainee. If the trainee is inexperienced and insecure, the technique could at first be carefully prescribed so that he learns acceptable techniques with little confusion. This highly controlled situation may also be used to develop skills that have a high incidence of success and where there is no point in letting the trainee work them out for himself.

The unspecified form of situation allows flexibility for the trainee and is more like the school situation. This sort of practice situation is more appropriate after the trainee has acquired several modes of behavior and feels at ease in the training situation. The kind of condition with which the student is to begin cannot be specified apart from the circumstances in a particular case. A few examples will help clarify the above distinctions. Consider the following controlled simulated situation:

A group of disadvantaged children is assembled, some half dozen. The teacher in training is told to present a given explanation to the group. One member of the group has been asked to make a drumming noise on his desk as the teacher is working with them. The specified behavior is a task focus-technique in which the teacher recognizes the noise and directs attention to the need to complete the work.

This simulated situation could easily be converted into one with a high degree of flexibility by simply not specifying the technique.

Consider next a real situation in which the behavior is prescribed:

A group of disadvantaged children is assembled and the teacher is told that he is to teach a particular concept. The prescribed behavior of the teacher is as follows: Present three characteristics that identify the concept. Then present two instances of the category and mention two or three other objects, some belonging to the category and some not. Ask the pupils which of the objects is included in the concept.

It is clear that this situation is highly structured. But it would be flexible were the trainee told to teach the particular concept and decide the procedure for himself.

A fully developed program of training requires a massive supply of situations prepared with far more care than was taken in the cases above. It is not easy to find training situations in educational literature. The following examples are taken from research literature and approximate the sort of elaboration that an instructional program would require.

EXAMPLE 1. This practice situation partially develops the ability to perform stimulant operations by giving practice in four skills. These are skills in inducing pupils to clarify, in evoking critical awareness, in refocusing pupil response, and in prompting.

Today you will have an opportunity to develop skills in basic classroom questioning techniques. The session is designed to help you extend the range and quality of your questioning techniques in such a way that the pupils you teach are led to think more deeply about problems raised in class.

The techniques outlined below are designed to be used in discussion, review, and inductively organized lessons where active pupil participation is prerequisite to the realization of the goals of instruction. Any given technique may be appropriate in one situation but not in another. The selection of a particular technique depends upon the extent to which, in your judgment, it requires the pupil to analyze a problem critically or to justify rationally his answer. Do not use a given technique unless you feel it contributes to the educational relevance of the lesson.

Your goal is to ask penetrating and probing questions that require pupils to go beyond superficial, "first-answer" responses.

BASIC QUESTIONING TECHNIQUES: There are two ways of achieving the above goal: 1) The teacher asks penetrating questions that require pupils to get at the heart of the problem. This forestalls superficial answers. Whether you are able to do this largely depends upon your knowledge of relevant content; 2) The second approach is based on specific techniques that may be used *after* the pupil has responded in some way (i.e., a question, a comment, an answer to a teacher's question). The goal here is to get the pupil to go beyond his first response. You are attempting to produce greater critical awareness and depth by *probing*. Your cue is the pupil's response—once it has occurred, don't immediately go on with the discussion yourself. *Probe* his answer by means of one of the techniques outlined below.

I. *Teacher Seeks Further Clarification by the Pupil:* You may ask the pupil for more information and/or more meaning. You may respond to the pupil's responses by saying such things as:

a) "What do you mean?"
b) "Could you put that in other words to make clearer what you mean?"
c) "Can you explain that further?"
d) "What do you mean by the term . . . ?"

II. *Teacher Seeks Increased Pupil Critical Awareness:* Here you are requiring the pupil to justify his response rationally. You may say:

a) "What are you/we assuming here?"
b) "Why do you think that is so?"
c) "Have we/you oversimplified the issue—is there more to it?"
d) "Is this one or several questions?"
e) "How would someone who took the opposite point of view respond to this?"

III. *Teacher Seeks to Refocus the Pupil's Response:* If a pupil has given a high quality answer, it may seem unnecessary to *probe* it. However, you can *refocus* his or the class's attention on a related issue.

a) "Good! What are the implications of this for . . . ?"
b) "How does this relate to . . . ?"
c) "Can you take it from there and tie it into . . . ?"

IV. *Teacher Prompts Pupil:* In *prompting* you are giving the pupil a hint to help him go on and answer a question. Suppose a pupil has given an I-don't-know or I'm-not-sure type of response. Rather than giving him the answer or redirecting the question to another pupil, you may give the puzzled student a hint.

Teacher: "John, define the term 'polygenesis'."
John: "I can't do it."
Teacher: *(prompting)* "What does poly mean?" or, "Well, genesis means origin or birth, and poly means . . . ?"

This technique allows you to *probe* even though at first it appears that the pupil can't answer the question.

V. *Redirect:* This is not the *probing* technique per se. It helps you bring other students into the discussion quickly while still using *probing* techniques. In *redirecting,* you merely change the direction of interaction from yourself and the first pupil to yourself and the second pupil.

> Teacher: "What is the relationship between pressure and volume?"
>
> First Pupil: "As the pressure goes up, the gas is condensed."
>
> Teacher: (to Second Pupil) "Can you tell us what is meant by condensed?" Or, "Can you restate that in terms of volume?"

To sum up, the techniques outlined above have two things in common:

1. They are initiated by the teacher immediately after the pupil has responded.
2. They require the pupil to go beyond the information he has already given.

CONCLUDING REMARKS: Try to use the techniques as frequently as you can. Do not stay with one given technique for too long at one time. In addition, don't forget to reinforce when you *probe*— if you are not at ease you may otherwise behave like a "Philadelphia lawyer."

If you prefer to run through the first five-minute lesson as a warm-up, this would be fine. You may teach the same lesson over two or three times. We will focus more on *probing* than on transmitting new or complex material. The maximum amount of time for the session will be two hours.[2]

EXAMPLE 2. This situation contributes to the development of the ability to diagnose pupils' needs and errors. The skill is in identifying errors in long division and in prescribing remedial measures.

> Ten examples in long division solved by a pupil in the fifth grade are given to the trainee. He is asked to study the pupil's work and to identify the errors and indicate what he would do to remedy the pupil's tendency to make these mistakes.

The trainee's prescriptions may be evaluated by the trainer as being totally relevant, moderately relevant, or not relevant.[3]

EXAMPLE 3. This example may be used to develop the ability to judge appropriateness of materials. The skill is in judging the proper level of reading books for different pupils. The instructions to the trainee are:

> You are the teacher of Paul, Pam, Richard, and Connie. You are to select books for instruction in the classroom. You will hear each child read aloud (via video recording) the three selections which he has just finished reading silently. After each selection, decide if the material is too easy, appropriate, or too hard for that child's instruction in the classroom.

The number of words miscalled (say, one error for twenty running words) may be used as a rough criterion of difficulty in discussions with the trainee. But the cues used by the trainee should be focal points of discussion in the feedback sessions.[4]

These situations can be used with children of all cultural backgrounds and social origins. The first example is perhaps more suitable for training junior and senior high school teachers than for elementary teachers, although with appropriate modifications it could be used with teachers of the intermediate grades.

Many types of training exercises must be devised. Some are scattered through the pedagogical literature, and many have yet to be formulated. Perhaps one or two additional examples will give a rough idea of possible variations. An audio or video recording can be made of verbal exchanges in the classroom. The responses of the teacher to what pupils say can be cut out. As an illustration, consider the following excerpt from a tape recording:

Teacher: "And crimes are classified in what way?"
Pupil: "Well, the first one would be treason. Treason, and there is felony, and misdemeanors."
Teacher: "What's the meaning of treason?"
Pupil: "There are two subdivisions—sabotage or something like that."
Teacher: ————————————————————————

The trainees can be asked to make the next response to the pupil. These responses will vary, and their probable effects on the pupils can be discussed. On the basis of the discussion, the trainees may devise practice exercises to find out how pupils do actually respond to what they say.

To give another instance, much of the standard instructional material is probably inadequate for disadvantaged children. The teacher-to-be must learn to distinguish the material suitable for them. Perhaps his training should begin with judging the instructional utility of visual materials such as films and slides. Assume that he has been associated with a group of deprived children in other training situations. On the basis of his knowledge of them, the trainee would be asked to select a film or set of slides to be shown to the group. If the responses of the children are good, the instructor helps the trainee identify the qualities that made the materials effective. If the materials evoke negative or indifferent responses, the trainee would then study the materials, decide what his error was, discuss his ideas with the instructor, then test them by trying other selections.

The situations should cover a wide range of social backgrounds. Here are but a few illustrations of what some of these situations might entail: There should be training situations in which the trainee learns to talk with parents who were themselves failures in school and who now see no purpose in schooling for their children. He should learn to talk with parents who have hopes for their children but cannot articulate them, or who do not see how their hopes can be realized because of the discriminations and social circumstances of their lives. The training situation should provide for the development of skills for the teacher-to-be to identify himself with children who are educationally and socially disadvantaged, and to recognize when a child feels discriminated against. This is part of the affective preparation of the teacher and will be treated in the next chapter.

The curriculum procedure implicit in the training plan set forth in this chapter is simple and can be analyzed into the following phases:

1. The job of teaching is analyzed into the tasks that must be performed. (This phase was discussed in Chapter 5.)
2. The abilities required for the performance of these tasks must be specified.
3. The skills or techniques through which the abilities are expressed must be clearly described.
4. Training situations and exercises for the development of each skill must be worked out in detail.
5. Training situations and exercises should be classified and indexed by tasks, abilities, skills, grade levels, fields of instruction, and backgrounds of children.

The responsibility for the development of these training materials cannot be left solely to individual colleges and universities. The task is too great and the staff time and resources required are more extensive than a single institution can afford. The preparation of an adequate supply of instructional materials for the training of teachers can be done successfully—this must be emphasized—only by a massive effort supported by federal and state funds and incorporating the participation of universities, colleges, public schools, and the professional organizations of teachers.

The purpose of this supply of training situations is to increase the trainer's options and to provide an orderly program in which each ability receives proper emphasis. The resourceful training instructor will often devise new situations and adapt the ready-made ones to his liking.

There is now no set of training situations available to teacher educators. There are lists of objectives, tests for assessing the cognitive achievement and attitudes of trainees, and scales for rating their teaching behavior. There are all kinds of pretentious models for teacher education. But there are no materials to be used in actually training the teacher. As a result, the training of the teacher is carried on intuitively, haphazardly, and with little regard for the spectrum of abilities the trainee should have. If a person is poorly trained and must deal with problems by trial and error in complex and swiftly moving events, as in a classroom, he probably will be unhappy in his work. This fact, noted earlier, is perhaps related to the number of teachers who are dropouts from their profession.

Training and the Principle of Feedback

More is needed than just practice of a technique in a training situation if skill in its performance is to be developed. Feedback is also necessary. Many years ago Thorndike showed that not only practice but awareness of the consequences of one's behavior is necessary to its improvement. The current term is not "awareness of the consequences" but "feedback," a term taken from the study of servomechanisms.

When the sensitive teacher observes the effects of his actions in the faces, postures, eyes, and speech of the children, he is receiving feedback. What he does next is influenced by this information. When the teacher assesses an action and decides how to do it better or to try something else, he is acting in the light of feedback. The teacher who is not trained to observe the effects of his behavior does it intuitively and crudely.

The teacher also emits cues. These cues function in teaching because they are taken by pupils as indications of the teacher's attitudes. The posture of the teacher, the look in his eyes, or the frown on his face tell the pupil about his feelings and intentions. Feedback is at least a two-way track.

The trainee must be taught to analyze the teaching-learning situation as he teaches. This is too important to leave its improvement to chance. His ability to analyze the situation will largely determine the content of the feedback. He will learn how to analyze situations from his study of protocol materials involving diagnosis and reinforcement in the theoretical component of his training. This will be developed further in the training situations worked out for techniques of analysis and reinforcement.

This sort of feedback might be called primary feedback. It is what the teacher tells himself from his observations of what is going on about him. But there is another kind of feedback—a secondary kind. It comes from others and, in the training situation, from the teacher trainer. The instructor encourages, approves, and criticizes the trainee's performance. He uses the principle of feedback to shape the trainee's behavior to the specifications of the technique.

The kinds of feedback discussed above cannot be planned in advance as can the training situations. Neither trainees nor pupils will respond in the same way from one performance to another. Therefore, the information that can be fed back to the trainee cannot be predetermined. How, then, can the training instructor use the principle of feedback to help him shape the trainee's performance?[5] He can use this principle only if he has a record of the trainee's practice sessions. The teacher trainer must see that audio and video recordings of the trainee's behavior are made for more careful study. By analyzing the recorded material, the trainer can decide what aspects of the trainee's behavior are to be reinforced and how to do this. The teacher trainer would need to analyze the behavior of the trainee and pupils as it occurred on the recording before he begins to help the trainee improve his performance. From his study of the materials, the trainer would be able to raise questions that would help the trainee reflect upon his behavior. The trainer could also reinforce or extinguish the way certain questions were asked or the way the trainee responded to the behavior of the pupil.

Another way the consequences of the trainee's behavior could be fed back to him is by use of videotapes and films that present a high degree of skill in the performance of the technique. Viewing his own video recordings and comparing them with the more skilled performance, the trainee could modify his own teaching behavior.[6] The trainee should not imitate a model, nor study *it* instead of his own behavior, but gather information from it that will help him examine and change his behavior.

It has been shown in a number of studies that immediate feedback is more effective than delayed feedback. But this principle does not hold when the performance of the trainee can be replayed through tape and film. If a practice session is videotaped and played back to the trainee several days or weeks later, the effects are as great as if the feedback had immediately followed the original performance.[7] The video recording is able to recreate the situation so vividly that the trainee can re-live it and profit from the feedback. This allows the trainer to study the behavior of the trainee before discussing it with him. Feedback is only as good as the monitoring.

Moreover, successive practice sessions are a source of primary feedback for the teacher trainer. They give him an opportunity to assess the effectiveness of his training techniques.

Objections and Answers

At least three objections may be raised against the view of teacher training presented here. The first is that the term "training" is a bad word. To those who suffer from semantic afflictions, it is an insult to human intelligence because training is used to teach tricks to animals. To others "training" means a mechanical performance without a strong basis in theory. Training a teacher supposedly violates his individuality and makes him incapable of operating as a self-determining agent; it cripples his innovative capacity. This is a strange position because it is contradicted by everything known about training in other occupations. The trained surgeon or airplane pilot will perform his duties more successfully in an emergency than anyone else. A trained individual has relaxed control which frees him from preoccupation with immediate acts so he can scan the new situation and respond to it constructively. Training and resourcefulness are complementary, not antithetical, elements of behavior.

The second objection is that there are not enough tested techniques to form the basis of an explicit program. No one can deny that the effectiveness of most teaching skills has yet to be proved. These skills have been distilled from practical experience, enriched by research in psychology and philosophy; but only a few, such as techniques of teaching reading, spelling, and typing have been developed by research. The least dependable techniques can be weeded out with practical experience and theoretical knowledge. The remainder will be the initial stock of a viable store of pedagogical techniques. Research workers can test the effects of these techniques when there is a dependable way of training teachers. The effectiveness of skills cannot be established experimentally until teachers can be trained to perform them. Objecting to a training program because of lack of tested techniques is the same as denying the efficacy of any training program at all.

In the third place, it can be objected that the program of training proposed here has not been shown to be empirically superior to other ways of producing teachers. Of course this point is readily admitted. But this is a defeatist argument that carries little weight except in the field of education where it is the refuge of the "standpatter." Had it been listened to in other fields, progress would have been impeded just as it will be in teacher education. Nevertheless, some aspects of this program do have experimental support. It has been shown that feedback affects what the teacher and trainee do and that it is most effective when the trainee is aware of the behavior to which it is relevant.[8] It is also evident from research and practical experience that the abilities listed in the early part of this chapter are in fact those that teachers use as they teach, however crudely they may be performed.

But there is no conclusive evidence that any program of teacher training is superior to another, just as there is no conclusive evidence of a superior way to train physicians or engineers. So it is the better part of wisdom to provide explicit programs, carefully designed training materials, and to rely as little as possible upon haphazard instruction and incidental learning. Systematic instruction is a far better basis for subsequent self-correction and growth in skills.

CHAPTER 7

SHAPING THE AFFECTIVE ASPECTS
OF TEACHER BEHAVIOR

The teacher uses his pedagogical knowledge and skill and his knowledge of and about subject matter in teaching as we shall see in later chapters. His personality and attitudes are also involved. The purpose here is to analyze this latter aspect of teaching and suggest ways it may be shaped in a program of teacher preparation.

Role of Personality in Teaching

It is widely believed that the effectiveness of a teacher is dependent upon his personality: if a person knows his subject matter, he can learn to teach from a modicum of experience because teaching is basically an expression of his personality; failure to succeed after this preparation can be attributed to defects in personal style—he lacks charm, zeal, warmth, or sensitivity, or else he is authoritarian or too laissez faire.

When personality is relied upon as a substitute for training, it becomes a stumbling block to the development of programs of teacher preparation. But when it is considered as a complex of factors modifiable by instruction and for which a training program can be designed, it can be a very important facet of teacher preparation.

Before we go further, perhaps the term "personality" should be given a more definite meaning. The term is used in a number of ways. Some authorities use it to refer to a summary description of a person's total ways of behaving. Others use the term to designate constitutional characteristics such as being withdrawn or outgoing, thoughtful or unreflective, enthusiastic or apathetic. Still other authorities use the term "personality" to refer to an internal frame of reference consisting of self-evaluative feelings and attitudes regarding one's adequacy, worth, capacity, guilt, and so forth. Negative self-evaluations may lead an individual to defend himself in various ways. Some of these defense mechanisms may, and often do, influence his teaching behavior. These self-oriented attitudes are probably learned, although they may be shaped to some extent by constitutional factors. The internal frame of reference and its defense system, together with the constitutional style of behavior, we shall call personality.

The individual also has attitudes toward other persons and objects. He has feelings and evaluations about ethnic groups, school policies, teachers' unions, and so on. While these attitudes may be affected by his internal frame of reference, they do not necessarily entail self-evaluation. We are therefore separating them from self-oriented attitudes, and shall refer to them as other-oriented feelings and attitudes.

There can be no question that the teacher's personality does influence his teaching. But the significance of this fact can be, and often is, overemphasized. It is sometimes considered to be important enough to justify the selection of prospective teachers by their personality. The current tendency to reduce teaching to a craft, and thus require only a knowledge of subject matter and on-the-job experience, stems from a belief in the mystic power of personality, as well as from a lack of information about teaching behavior and what is required to develop it.

A more defensible view, and certainly one that is compatible with the position taken here, is that teacher preparation should be designed to help the prospective teacher use his own style of behavior to best advantage.[1] If a teacher is withdawn and reserved, he should be helped to interact with pupils in a more outgoing fashion, but one in keeping with his basic personal style.

Four dimensions of personality have been identified by Peck in his study of students in teacher education:
1. conscience-ruled stability versus unprincipled impulsiveness
2. creatively intelligent autonomy versus unthinking dependence
3. loving affection versus cold hostility
4. relaxed, outgoing optimism versus anxious, self-preoccupied pessimism[2]

From these dimensions and other considerations, Peck and his associates were led to conclude that a program of preparation of teachers should be adapted to personality types. In his view, this would not only be efficient but would also preserve the personal style of each prospective teacher. He suggests that a program of teacher preparation based upon specific skills taught in a similar fashion to all trainees would somehow produce a uniform style of teaching.[3]

The suggestion of these two approaches to the development of training programs seems to set up a dichotomy based upon differences concerning the role of personality in teaching. One view emphasizes specific skills and ignores, if it does not actually stamp out, idiosyncratic aspects of behavior. The other view emphasizes the personal style of each prospective teacher and attempts to provide him with the skills that make his style more effective.

This dichotomy is more apparent than real. No matter how much an individual may be trained in any particular skill, the style of the individual in classroom performance will neither be eliminated nor rendered ineffectual. Every activity has its artistic side. Football players are skilled in specific ways of tackling, yet no two individuals will tackle in precisely the same way. A medical student may practice tying surgical knots or making a particular incision for countless hours; nevertheless, each surgeon will have his own individual peculiarities in the performance of these skills. The idiosyncratic aspects of behavior will show up in the teacher's performance no matter how much he is trained in specific skills. There is a limited sense in which every individual is to his manner born. As suggested earlier, the individual who has command of specific skills will have enough relaxed control over a particular teaching situation to perform in his natural style. These two approaches to the development of programs of teacher education are not in opposition as is sometimes claimed, but in fact, complementary. One without the other will yield an incomplete program.

Teaching the Prospective Teacher to Manage Himself

Any program of teacher preparation should help a prospective teacher with his personality problems, because these may, and often do, prevent the teacher from interacting effectively with pupils, peers, parents, and other members of the community. For example, a teacher may have a tendency to break into the discourse of his pupils, interrupting their thoughts and giving them the impression that he is aggressive. He may be habituated to smiling, even in inappropriate situations. He may set perfective standards for himself. He may be overanxious to be liked by his pupils, or he may be hampered by feelings of inadequacy. These aspects of his personality will most certainly affect his teaching behavior no matter how skilled he may be in techniques of teaching or how knowledgeable he may be in his subject of instruction.

Peck and his associates give the following example of how a teacher's personality may affect his pupils. The case is one in which a new teacher tries to avoid being disliked by overindulging a pupil of whom she is fond. The following exchange between two teachers takes place:

> First Teacher: But I haven't moved him away from his friends. I told him to find a place where he thought he could do his work. If he sat on the chandelier, I'd just love it if he would pay attention. He says, "Why are you always picking on me?" I said, "You're the one I see talking. But you contribute so much when you do contribute." I told him it's constant turmoil and I just can't have it.

> Second Teacher: Maybe he knows you are fond of him and he can get away with a little bit.

> First Teacher: (sighs) It would be so easy if I didn't like him. So easy to tell him to sit down and shut up, but I'm afraid I'm going to hurt his feelings and squander the little initiative he has.

> Second Teacher: Maybe it's not *his* feelings so much . . .[4]

The teacher apparently is afraid to exercise control over the pupil for fear of driving him to show dislike of her, an action which would fly in the face of her need of him. It seems evident from this exchange that the teacher's difficulty arises neither from her lack of skill in conducting the classwork nor lack of command of the subject matter, but from her inability to understand and control herself.

Self-management involves the control of feelings and attitudes that the teacher has toward himself. He is not always aware of these feelings and attitudes. They are sometimes unpleasant, so he does not like to face them. But the teacher who comes to terms, as nearly as possible, with his own self-realities will be one who increases control over himself and the teaching situation.

One of the primary functions of a program of teacher preparation is to help the prospective teacher become aware of his self-oriented feelings and attitudes and be increasingly able to cope with them. Among the self-feelings and attitudes that a preparatory program should deal with are the following: feelings about one's own limitations; the need to be liked, to be approved of by pupils and peers; feelings of inferiority; feelings of insecurity; paranoid tendencies: suspicion and fear of pupils.

The prospective teacher typically does not know his limitations. He is likely not to know, for instance, how he will react in situations of stress or in situations where excessive affection is shown him by pupils. His resistance to affection may be so low that he becomes involved in innocent but embarrassing relations that may damage a pupil as well as himself. He may become confused under stress and unable to make decisions; or he may assume an aggressive attitude and behave in ways he will later regret. In such situations it is just as important for the teacher to be sensitive to his own inner feelings and reactions, and to respond to them constructively, as it is for him to make appropriate reactions to others who are involved in the situation with him.

Most teachers need to be liked by their pupils as well as by their peers. This is especially true of beginning teachers. The prospective teacher, however, may not be aware of how strong this need for approval really is in himself. He may often do things to fulfill this need that are in fact detrimental to either himself or his pupils. In some cases, as was seen above, his need to be liked may be in conflict with his responsibility for exercising control over his pupils. Or, to cite another example, a teacher's need for status and approval among his peers may be so great that he overplays his ingratiating behavior, causing his peers to withdraw from him, thus increasing his need for approval rather than reducing it. A teacher may act in the same way toward his pupils by being oversolicitous. He may yield to their unjustified complaints about overwork and take undue measures to please them.

Almost every beginning teacher feels insecure as he confronts a group of pupils. The prospective teacher is concerned about his ability to get along in the classroom. He does not know what sorts of questions he will be asked nor how he will answer them. He cannot foresee the kinds of misconduct that may arise in the class, and, if he did foresee them, he would scarcely know how to deal with them. Even though the teacher may have been fairly well trained in the techniques of dealing with pupils under varying conditions, he will still feel insecure when he faces a group of children for whom he alone is responsible.

Insecurity may arouse feelings of inferiority and drive the teacher to be overconcerned with himself. A teacher so preoccupied is less likely to concern himself with the needs of his pupils. If the teacher feels that he is accepted by his peers, his supervisors, and his pupils, he will be better able to assess pupil behavior and the various situations with which he must cope. But in the face of insecurity, a teacher may react in ways that are harmful to children. The following illustrates how an insecure teacher reacted to a child who may have cheated:

Barbara S. said she wasn't sure the child had cheated; there was no way to prove it. She was afraid that in case he had, and the other children knew it, the class would look down on her for not being smart enough to catch him. If he hadn't and she accused him, his parents might come down and complain to the principal. So she decided to imply she knew he had cheated, without actually saying so, to protect herself in case he had.

The child surely felt devalued by the insinuation that he had cheated, but he could neither defend himself nor make restitution. The teacher was, understandably, concerned with herself and her own security. She was afraid of censure, of admitting she did not know whether or not the child had cheated. She could not even begin to understand the child because she did not feel free enough to have an unsolved problem on her hands, to say, "I am not sure, I do not know."[5]

In addition to the feelings and attitudes the prospective teacher may have toward himself, there are generalized and free-floating anxieties that may interfere with his performance. If he suffers from paranoid tendencies, he is likely to have a generalized fear of pupils and be suspicious of them. When these tendencies are heightened by pupil behavior or by the behavior of the teacher's peers, they may seriously interfere with his perception of the classroom circumstances. He may make all sorts of erroneous diagnoses, and follow courses of action which intensify whatever difficulties he had in the first place.

The feelings the teacher has toward himself are ordinarily not affected, or at least not very much, by increasing his skill in the techniques of teaching and classroom control, or in working with his peers and members of the community. If the teacher is to become aware of those aspects of his personality which are turned in upon himself, he will need the help of a counselor. Sometimes the problems of the individual teacher can best be handled in individual counseling sessions. At other times group counseling may be more appropriate. It is important for the teacher in training to become aware of the fact that others are having similar feelings and attitudes and that there are differences in style of performance among teachers even though they employ the same techniques.

It will often be advisable for the counselor and students to have access to tape recordings and films of each prospective teacher's classroom performance. The trainee may need to observe what he is doing and know how children are responding to him when his behavior is affected by self-oriented feelings and attitudes. As he reviews a film of his teaching performance, the trainee is often able to profit from his own analysis as well as from the feedback of his counselor. The following example is taken from a report by Peck and his associates and shows how a trainee's penchant for perfection may be an obstruction to his classroom performance. This particular teacher has been working with a counselor for several sessions. Her classroom work has been filmed and recorded, and the following is part of the discourse covered by a segment of the film:

Teacher: O.K., I'm going to give you the directions to find this place. First of all, 88° south latitude, 110 east. Approximately 110 east, it's an island, so I can't give you just one.

Pupil: What was that south?

Teacher: It's approximately 8°.

Pupil: 8°? You said 88.

Teacher: I meant 8°. I didn't say it right. Approximately 8° south. It's an island, a very famous island. . . The word for the island is synonymous with another word for coffee, and there has been a song written about it. O.K., what is it?

Pupil: Java.

Teacher: Java, the island of Java. Yes, Jim?

Pupil: Wasn't your latitude wrong? You said 8° south.

Teacher: It's not? What is it?

Pupil: It's 8° north, I mean about 10 or 12° north.

Teacher: No, it isn't.

Pupil: You look and you will see it is.

Teacher: Look on that one map, and don't look at it another way.

Pupil: I was in a different place.

Teacher: Well, if I was wrong, you should have corrected me, and this time I was right. O.K.[6]

In this teacher's conference with her counselor, she indicates something of the change that has come about in her feelings concerning this particular sort of incident. The following is a discussion between the counselor and the teacher:

Counselor: One thing I noticed in this test material you filled out is that you are real introspective, in that you evaluate what you do, think about it, saying that "Well, I'm beginning to get too assertive," you used the word aggressive.

Teacher: Well, my whole experience points toward that. Everything since I graduated from college would lead me to be introspective, I think, if I had the inclination to be anything. I think it would have naturally pointed me that way. I think it is wonderful, because I can't see doing things and having actions that you are not really aware of. In other words, if I am mad or something, I know I'm mad. For instance, Friday I had graded everything wrong, I had made a mistake in my grading. My grading was proper, but the way it was done was not proper; I didn't know it. I had to go back and go through a lot of bother and it made me feel like an idiot. Fortunately, my co-partner had done the same thing, so it was the two of us. I wasn't alone in my idiocy. So I went back and changed everything. That afternoon I was gripey and fussy with everyone I talked to; I was very mad. I finally just admitted, "Johnny, I have just made an idiot out of myself at school, and I was just mad. And I'll just be mad all afternoon."

Counselor: It helps to have someone to talk to.

Teacher: It sure does. To the kids one day in school, I'll always have the tendency to go "uh-huh." I did that one day and the whole class went "uh-huh" back to me! I just asked them, do I do that all the time? They said "yes"; I said, well, I hadn't realized that it was as obvious as that. So I kind of, well, I'm more open now to listening to people talk about me, and for me to talk about myself. Admit what I'm angry about, and it also appears very foolish to be mad three hours later about an incident.

Counselor: I think this is a big change in you, that you used to be kind of introspective, and it kind of had you trapped, and now it doesn't. You can call yourself an idiot, but you didn't have the same feelings that you would have had a year ago.

Teacher: No, I take it a lot more in stride now than I would have a year ago. I used to be very, well, had to succeed at all costs. Be A-Number One in whatever I did, which obviously, not accepting my limitations, you know. And now, I can accept them, and feel kind of good that I have them. There is nothing shameful in admitting that I did something wrong. I made a mistake, it's natural. I caught other people doing what I would now admit to, without them admitting to it themselves. I see myself a lot of times over; and I'm very glad that I don't have to be embarrassed or feel guilty because I couldn't succeed in something.

Counselor: So much communication going on that you knew you didn't have to prove it, that they knew you were on the ball as much as you could be.

Teacher: It's when they accept you as being competent and able and if you make a mistake, you're able to correct it and go on.

Counselor: How does this work in the classroom, this attitude of yours?

Teacher: To make mistakes? It doesn't bother me, because, for instance, at first, I was very, very afraid to give any kind of evaluation of myself, but I knew, my mind knew that it was the only sensible way to get any sort of feedback, because I had seen it practiced in lots of classrooms, and I was so scared to open and read my mistakes, but a lot of the evaluations said you don't use film enough, so I started using more films. By making mistakes, that's kind of an indirect way, but if I make a mistake, then I make a mistake. Kids shouldn't think that I'm not a person; they are inclined to see a teacher as something similar to God, not ordinary people like their parents. Now, that's not right, teachers are people, too.

Counselor: Then they can accept their mistakes better.

Teacher: Yes, if I'm an adult and they think I'm halfway reasonable and say if I make a mistake, you don't see me cry over it. Then hopefully, they will do the same thing too, as they grow up and be freer and more open themselves.

Counselor: And your responsibility which shows all through is so solid that it doesn't need to be spoken. They know you're going to do something about your mistakes.

Teacher: That's different. I've always been able to do something about my mistakes, but now I do it with a different attitude. It doesn't crush me."[7]

There are many kinds of situations that involve the teacher's feelings and attitudes toward himself. This case is a simple indication of how important it is for a program of teacher preparation to provide help for the trainee to come to terms with himself as he works into the role of a professional teacher.

Feelings and attitudes do not flow in one direction. The pupils also have feelings and attitudes toward the trainee, as well as toward other objects and aspects of their environment. The trainee is often unaware of them. To sensitize him to these feelings and to help him to see how his own behavior affects them is to lay the groundwork for improving the trainee's ability to control his own behavior. There are various ways of helping the trainee recognize his pupils' feelings and attitudes. One of these is to sensitize him to the emotional significance of the verbal and nonverbal expressions of his pupils. This can be done through the use of films of teaching performance. In some cases feelings and attitudes must be inferred solely from pupil behavior. When it is possible, it is desirable for the pupil to view the film and recount to a counselor how he felt at the time. The results of this session can be used to verify the trainee's interpretation of the pupil's feelings. Many films of this type can be prepared and used over and over again with trainees. The possible kinds of situations and techniques that can be used in preparing the teacher to control himself and to understand the emotional behavior of children and youths are extensive. The preparation of materials for this purpose is one of the most pressing tasks in the development of programs of teacher preparation.

Other-Oriented Attitudes

The teacher-to-be naturally has feelings and attitudes toward children. As he begins to work in the training complex and to participate in school work, he will also exhibit attitudes toward his peers, his supervisors, and the community. These are often more specific and more openly expressed than the *self*-oriented attitudes. They are directed toward particular individuals or groups and to specific social or educational policies and practices. The trainee may:

—have dislikes for, or be fond of, particular pupils,
—dislike particular ethnic groups,
—be more favorably disposed toward docile pupils,
—be more inclined toward acceptance of compliant and withdrawn behavior than toward aggressive and blatant behavior,
—view disadvantaged children as unstable and lacking the qualities required in formal schooling,
—believe that the failure of a child from a minority ethnic group is a result of his inadequate capacity to learn, or
—have low expectations of children of poverty.

These are only a few of the feelings and attitudes that can reduce the effectiveness of a teacher. Almost all trainees will harbor some attitudes such as these.

Many classroom difficulties stem from the fact that the teacher's attitudes are often in conflict with those of his pupils. Children whose cultural motivations are quite different from those of the teacher often behave in ways unacceptable to him. The attitudes of the teacher toward order and authority in the classroom, for example, often run counter to the ordinary behavior to which the child of poverty is accustomed. When the teacher attempts to control pupil behavior in accordance with his own attitudes, clashes between himself and his pupils are likely to occur.

As noted in an earlier chapter, a teacher's expectations will definitely influence what, and how well, his pupils do. If he is suspicious of a pupil, or thinks so poorly of him that he expects little or no achievement, the teacher, by this very fact, tends to create conditions that impede the pupil's learning. There is perhaps no attitude of the teacher that debilitates a pupil more than low expectation. It is more often directed toward the children of poverty than toward any other group.

One of the basic tasks of those responsible for designing programs of teacher education is to work out ways to help the trainee become aware of his attitudes, and to provide situations that will cause the trainee to reflect upon his attitudes and effect changes in them.

Helping the Prospective Teacher
Improve His Attitudes

Other-oriented attitudes consist of at least two components: feeling and cognition. The strength of these components varies with the nature of the attitude. Some attitudes consist almost entirely of feeling, others are largely cognitive. Between these two extremes are attitudes composed of varying degrees of each of these two components. If a teacher does something simply because he likes a pupil —lets a pupil work at drawing instead of doing his arithmetic—he is acting from an attitude that is almost entirely feeling. But if he lets him draw because the pupil excels in arithmetic and does not need to do further work on it, his attitude is primarily cognitive.

An attitude that is made up primarily of feeling, especially if it is rooted in some basic element of the trainee's personality such as his need for affection, can best be changed through counseling procedures, as we saw in the foregoing discussion. On the other hand, attitudes that are heavily weighted with cognitive elements can be approached through the examination of their content—reasons and evidence used to justify them, together with their relations to other attitudes held by the trainee.

Attitudes can be modified through an analytic approach.[8] One analytic procedure consists of raising an issue, let us say an issue in which a teachers' strike is involved; in group discussion, the prejudices of various trainees are elicited and either projected on a screen or written on a blackboard. Some of these will be for and some against strikes. These projected statements of attitudes can then be made the object of study and analysis. The fact that they are projected gives them a certain objectification; they become separated from the individuals who expressed them and can be looked at more impersonally.

The analysis will consist of an examination of what is assumed to be true about teachers' strikes. These assumptions can then be examined by reference to the accuracy of the information used to support them. Suppose that one of the assumptions is that strikes are not suited to a profession. In defense of this, a trainee may point out that people who strike very often resort to violence to attain their ends, and, in the course of a strike, they may attack those who cross picket lines and, in many cases, attempt to destroy property. When these efforts to justify the negative attitude toward teachers' strikes are then objectified by being put on exhibit before the group, they should be studied to ascertain their truth or to see how they are justified. This will lead to an examination of the facts about strikes and the context within which they occur. Each justification can be tracked down to its empirical and logical validity. In this way the cognitive grounds of the attitude will come under close scrutiny.

The justification of the attitude should also be examined from the standpoint of its consistency with principles of justice which the trainees hold. This may mean an examination of the concepts of freedom and equality, property rights, and individual rights. What is involved here is the extent to which the justification of the attitude is consistent with the large generalizations about what is just and right in society at large.

The approach suggested here is one in which the attitudes that have been exhibited are put between the jaws of a vise. One "jaw" is the factual evidence that can be accumulated and the other, the moral ideas of the individual or those underlying the institutional system. When an attitude is squeezed between these two jaws, it is likely to begin cracking. One round of study and criticism of this nature will seldom be sufficient to modify seriously the attitude of a trainee. But if this approach is used every time the opportunity arises, the attitude will in time appear to have so many faults that the trainee will hold it less tenaciously. No one is comfortable with an attitude which he knows to be incompatible with the facts or inconsistent with one's moral ideas. In time, such an attitude will be extensively modified if not abandoned.

It should be pointed out that while factual information and logical consistency with moral principles have a persuasive influence upon the trainee's attitudes, their influence is heightened when they come from sources the trainee is favorably disposed to.[9] For example, if he looks on majority opinion more favorably than expert opinion, he may be impressed by the results of opinion polls. Even so, he should learn to distinguish between what the majority thinks is right and what is held to be right and just in our historic traditions. Furthermore, when issues involving group norms are being considered, the influence of group deliberation upon the trainee will be stronger if he feels attached to the group and takes an active part in its concerns.[10]

The Need for a Systematic Program

The prospective teacher's attitudes and feelings are too important to leave the shaping of them to the accidents of human association or to the interests of individual instructors. A definite plan for identifying personality problems and attitudes should be developed in every program of teacher education. These problems and attitudes should be identified in the early stages of each trainee's preparation. And a systematic program of remedial situations should be worked out and followed through. This means that instructional situations and techniques should be prepared in advance for the various types of problems and attitudes. To do this will require the development of extensive amounts of diagnostic and instructional materials, as much, perhaps, as will be needed for training in the techniques of teaching. There is a great deal of talk about the importance of personality and attitudes in teaching, but there is a complete lack of instructional materials for doing anything about the development of proper attitudes and wholesome self-assessment and control. It is imperative that these materials be prepared at the earliest moment and that those who are involved in teacher education be trained in the use of them.

CHAPTER 8

THE TRAINING COMPLEX

The theoretical component of the training program can best be given in a university or college because there the student can concentrate on the structure of teaching while he is studying the substantive component of his preparation. In addition, the university or college staff is oriented toward the theoretical. But the training program calls for a new institutional mechanism because university personnel and existing facilities are inadequate.

First of all, the training program will require easy access to children, youth, and adults who represent a wide variety of cultural orientations and racial origins. Universities and colleges can reach far too few of these people, given their present resources. A university faculty is also too removed from the practicalities of teaching and running a school to operate a training program alone. But neither can the *schools* alone carry on a program. They cannot free enough children from classrooms to maintain an adequate training schedule. Besides, the schools do not have the theoretical resources and technical knowledge to sustain a program of training.

Functions of the Training Complex

These facts indicate the need for a new social mechanism with easy access to the schools and the universities. This is presently found in an incipient form under various names: cooperative teaching center, teaching techniques laboratory, or teacher education center.[1] Any of these titles is acceptable, of course. But these centers may also become places for the training of many kinds of service personnel: social workers, juvenile police, counselors, recreation supervisors, and school psychologists, as well as teachers. For this reason they are referred to here as training complexes. These complexes can exist only with the cooperation, influence, and participation of existing educational institutions and social agencies. They can serve a number of training functions for personnel at all levels of training and experience and at all levels of the educational structure.

No one can foresee all the functions such a complex will ultimately perform, but in its formative period it should serve as a place for:

—developing, preparing, and storing materials for training (practice specifications, video recordings of teaching, transcripts of classroom discourse, etc.)

—training new professional teachers in the skills entailed by the list of minimal abilities (See Chapter 6.)

—workshops, institutes, and conferences for the preparation of auxiliary teaching personnel

—institutes, workshops, and training laboratories for the continuing education of teachers

—courses, seminars, and workshops in subject matter fields relevant to the teacher's preparation or to the preparation of teacher aides and other auxiliary teaching personnel

To fulfill these functions, the complex must include a professional library of instructional resources (books, pamphlets, pictures, films, slides, etc.) for use with pupils at all grade levels. It must also have all sorts of technological equipment (kinescopes, video equipment, recorders, projectors, etc.) to be used in training teachers.

The Role of the Community*

The community should play an important role in the organization and operation of the training complex not only because such participation will help create a better complex but also because the complex may itself serve as a demonstration of the ways in which schools and universities can cooperate effectively with community groups.

There has been an almost revolutionary change in the relationships between school and community. Traditionally, it was the school that made educational plans, interpreted them to the community, and then tried to use the community as a resource in achieving educational goals. Today, an increasing number of communities want to participate actively in formulating educational plans. They want to communicate these hopes to the school and use the school's resources in achieving the community's goals.

Communities are generally unwilling these days to play a subservient role in the operation of the schools their children attend. They are no longer willing to accept projects, demonstrations, and

* This section was prepared by Harry N. Rivlin, School of Education, Fordham University.

experiments imposed upon them by schools or universities if they have no real voice in planning and in conducting the program. In these days of militancy, moreover, with militant youth, militant students, militant teachers, militant civil rights activists, and militant everybody else, community dissatisfaction with educational programs planned and conducted by outsiders is often expressed in militant opposition rather than in quiet grumbling.

Though it is important that the community play a responsible part in planning and conducting the training complex, this is often more easily said than done. Even a university which is most sympathetic with the needs of the community and is eager to get the help of the population it serves may find it difficult actually to work together with members of the community because college professors and militant leaders think differently and operate differently. For example, at most faculty committee meetings, people are eager to arrive at a consensus that satisfies all the objections that have been raised during a discussion, but a militant group that has learned how to use pressure to get what it is demanding does not see much to be gained by compromising and agreeing.

Because the underprivileged have found that what they get as a result of a change is often much less than has been promised, they tend to look suspiciously at any new proposal that is presented to them ready-made. Faculty people have to learn, therefore, how to involve community members early in the planning stage rather than later, and how to demonstrate their own sincerity rather than merely talk about it.

Another complication arises from the difficulty of learning what the community wants, and who speaks for the community. The essential feature of an urban community is the very diversity of its population. To think of the community as consisting only of the ghetto and the slum will alienate the middle class and will eventually turn the city into one vast ghetto slum. To ignore the ghetto and the slum community is equally unthinkable. Stereotypes, moreover, are almost totally irrelevant. There is no single picture of the slum child or parent that fits all of them, for children and parents in the slums differ as much among themselves as do middle class children and parents. To understand a community one must know the stresses that are tearing it apart as well as the forces that are keeping it together.

In short, universities which prepare educational personnel for urban schools must develop much greater understanding of the urban population, with all its shadings from rich to poor, with all its variations ethnically, religiously, and culturally. Failure to develop this understanding will almost inevitably lead to failure to develop the new educational procedures and the new kinds of educational personnel that are needed if urban education is to solve its problems and take advantage of its opportunities and resources.

Organization of the Training Complex

The organization of training complexes to meet the nation's demand for educational personnel will be difficult. There will arise questions of how many complexes are needed and where they should be located, how the complexes can be staffed, and where the pupils for training sessions will come from.

The training complex should be established as a joint enterprise by the public schools, universities and colleges, the community, and related public agencies. The university or college that attempts to extend its activities into a community, rich or poor, without the active involvement of the community leaders is almost certain to fail. The desires, expectations, and feelings expressed through the community's leaders must be reflected in the establishment and operation of a training complex. In short, the community must have some sense of ownership of the center or it will neither be welcomed nor long tolerated.

It is not possible to foresee how these complexes may ultimately be organized, controlled, and administered. However, there should be an advisory board made up of representatives from the various agencies involved in the complex and from the community at large. The members should be appointed and their terms staggered to preserve continuity from year to year. This board could serve as the machinery through which the interests and points of view of the various agencies and community groups are represented as the policies and programs of the complex are being developed.

Care must be taken to distinguish between technical questions which can be answered only by a professional and those of public interest because they directly affect the welfare of the community. Questions about how teachers should be trained to deal with cause-effect relations or interpersonal relationships, for example, are technical. On the other hand, the source of pupils for a training program in the complex is a subject the advisory board should consider. Decisions about the use of children and adults as subjects in a training program should be scrutinized by a board on which community members sit.

At the present time, training centers and laboratories are springing up all over the nation. But they tend to be poorly planned and inadequately staffed, and they lack a clear conception of the training function they are to perform. Such a center too easily becomes merely a new base for the traditional program of student teaching, with a few new catch phrases and gimmicks and a lot of fanfare about school participation. If ever there was a time when insightful planning for teacher training was needed, it is now. The federal government is poised to spend more millions of dollars on the training of teachers. Universities and colleges are rising to meet the growing demands for educational personnel. Public schools are making every effort to enter the field of teacher education. Yet all these resources are in danger of being used to bolster up old programs disguised as revolutionary developments by catchwords and empty phrases. Even at this late hour, state departments of public instruction, the various organizations of colleges and universities, and associations of school administrators in cooperation with the United States Office of Education could put order into what threatens to be a chaotic development. The leadership of these organizations and agencies could establish guidelines for deciding the location, control, and support of training complexes.

Any one of three different approaches could be followed in influencing the development of these centers of training. First, the development of training complexes could be left to the initiative of local institutions and communities. The guidelines would then be used by local groups in developing a training complex, as well as by funding agencies, in determining whether support should be given to the complex. Secondly, state and regional leadership might take on the responsibility of studying the needs of the region for training complexes and make recommendations about their location, control, and support. And third, a commission could be established to study the nation's need for training complexes and to make recommendations about their number, location, and support.

It is not feasible here to suggest which of these approaches is most likely to be successful. But local and regional interests should be incorporated and utilized to the fullest extent, no matter what plan is followed. The approach or approaches finally adopted will become a basis for federal and state appropriations in support of teacher training and for the cooperation of schools and higher institutions in developing and operating training programs.

Federal and state money for education should be used to solve national and local problems as well as to support the schools. It should not be used for increasing the income of the privileged or underwriting the economy. Legislation and financing should follow planning and not the other way around. The use of public money to encourage all sorts of schemes for dealing with crucial educational problems in the name of innovation, creativity, and pluralism is monstrous. It is especially so in a nation with enormous resources and talents for planning.

The Staff of a Complex

The task of staffing a training complex is beset with difficulties that stem from attitudes of college faculties and from the fears of school people about the interests of universities. In recent years the universities and colleges have tended to engage in public projects only when there was promise of research returns on the investment. Improvement in the services of social institutions has been of secondary interest. This orientation of higher institutions has led to a great deal of skepticism among teachers and school administrators about the benefits of cooperating with colleges and universities in the training of teachers. They fear that research will remain more important to the universities than the training function. University and college faculties, on the other hand, are inclined to believe that teachers and administrators are interested in superficial answers and mere practicalities. They fear that any effort to cooperate with teachers and administrators will end in frustration or lead to watered-down programs of education. There is probably some truth in what both sides believe and fear. Yet there are no differences between them that shared responsibilities and interactions cannot dispel.

Besides the prejudices separate faculties of the schools and colleges fear from one another, there is the problem of where to find the training personnel for the complexes. A considerable number of staff members should be elementary and secondary teachers, chosen not because they occupy a particular position, rate highly with administrators, or hold advanced degrees, but because they have the ability to train teachers. They should be effective teachers, articulate about what they do and why they do it. They should be able to demonstrate techniques of teaching and the use of criteria for the selection of instructional materials. And they should be competent in conferences with parents and teachers.

The staff members from the universities should include personnel from various fields and levels of instruction who are skilled in the techniques of teacher training. These representatives should be well disciplined in the analysis of teaching performance, the behavior of children, and the different forms of knowledge that appear in teacher-pupil discourse.

The commitment of the staff to the training function must be explicit and firm. The complex is a training center, not a research facility, and its staff must be competely devoted to the ideal of training. The reward system of the complex must be focused on performance of the training function and not on research and publication. The practice of encouraging classroom teachers and trainers of teachers to do research is too likely to amount to a prostitution of the teaching and training functions, at least until the dignity and complexity of these two functions become much more generally understood than at present.

Sources of Pupils and Clients

Second only to the problem of staffing is the question of where the pupils involved in the training program are to come from. Not enough pupils can be freed from classroom work to supply the needs of a training complex. And training in the strict sense can be given in the classroom only to a small degree. In order to run a training complex it is necessary to recruit pupils from community sources as well as the schoolroom. There are many unemployed dropouts and youths recently out of high school who could be employed to serve as pupils. This arrangement would offer employment to a considerable number of young people who cannot now find jobs. These youngsters could become interested in learning and even acquire new motivation from their work. A few teacher aides might be recruited from their number and some might even go on to become certified teachers or high-level professional workers.

In addition, the trainees are themselves a ready supply of pupils. While they are peers in training, they are not so in knowledge. A trainee in the teaching of mathematics could practice by teaching mathematics to his non-math peers, and similarly the trainee in English, science, and so on. While this procedure has obvious disadvantages, circumspect use of it could be a valuable supplement where other sources are insufficient.

Since an adequate number of elementary pupils cannot be supplied by the schools, the problem can be solved in two ways. With proper safeguards and the cooperation of parents, elementary school children could be employed as pupils after school hours and on Saturdays. The training complexes could also be operated during the summer when the number of available elementary school children is larger. Particularly in cases where children are having learning difficulties, which could be taken into account in planning the trainee's practice situations, the child's extra learning would be an added dividend. Furthermore, parents could also be employed as clients in training the teacher in techniques of empathy and communication.

A large number of illiterate or near-illiterate adults and young people could be employed as pupils and taught basic skills and certain elementary content. As a teacher of these pupils, the trainee could learn the techniques of teaching reading, arithmetic, language arts, and content subjects. In working with adults the trainee would miss certain experiences that can come only from teaching children, but he would still learn techniques of teaching.

A fringe benefit of employing members of the community as pupils and clients is the feeling of involvement they may come to have. As more and more people have experience in the complex, understand its purposes and procedures, and witness its adaptation to their own concerns and aspirations, community support will grow stronger.

Ultimately the complex could become a place where a wide spectrum of educational and social personnel (social workers, police, school psychologists, etc.) receive part of their training.

As teacher trainees become proficient in the training situations, they could begin to work with small groups in the schools. The number of skills the trainee should acquire prior to that would depend upon the judgment of his instructors and the opportunities the schools could make available. After his training with small groups he could take on entire classrooms. The purpose of working in the classroom and in small group situations is not to provide experience in the regular work of the school; it is to provide opportunities to find out where the trainee needs further instruction and training. The involvement of the student in school situations is not to be considered student teaching. As indicated earlier, student teaching is not training but a type of reality experience in which the individual learns by trial and error and by the inadequate direction that the supervising staff is able to give him. Student teaching came into being before the concept of training was developed and should be phased out as quickly as possible.

Intern Program

The purpose of training is to develop sufficient skills in teaching and handling group situations to enable the trainee to begin his teaching career as an intern. After completing his work in the training complex, the individual should be directly employed in a school system as an intern, not as a student teacher. He should no longer be subject to instruction by a university staff or the staff of the training complex, but be a charge of the school system in which he works.

An intern is one who enters professional practice under supervision after a period of training in the knowledge and techniques of his profession. There are now no true intern programs in teaching, only pseudo-programs, and few of these require prior preparation in the field of teaching. The MAT (Master of Arts in Teaching) programs not only require no preparation but reduce all pedagogical work to a pseudo-internship and related seminars. Those that do require previous preparation include no training, only conventional courses plus student teaching. Almost all combine on-the-job experience with seminars in problems of teaching or related topics, for the truth is that these so-called internships are at best only apprenticeships.

A proposal is made here for a genuine internship: a period of residence in a school system preceded by a well-defined, systematic program of training in the knowledge and skills of teaching. One condition is essential to the success of an intern program. The teacher with whom the intern works must be qualified and given sufficient time to work with the interns under his charge. The intern's work should receive close attention at all times and the remuneration of the supervisor must be made commensurate with the importance of the work.

Of course, there are probably not enough first-rate teachers to supply the demand for supervisors of interns. The training and preparation of supervisory personnel is a primary responsibility of the universities and colleges, especially those capable of providing high quality advanced work in education and its related disciplines. If institutions of higher learning concentrate upon the preparation of supervisory personnel to work with interns in the public schools, an adequate supply of supervisors could be provided in a relatively short time.

Any realistic survey of the situation will show that many interns must be placed in schools of mediocre quality. This condition will hardly be remedied in the near future. The problems that medical schools have had in placing their interns in satisfactory hospitals are well known. The problem in education is more severe because of the number of interns who will be involved in proportion to the number of high quality educational systems. Even so, trained supervisors of interns can go a long way toward producing good teachers in schools with less than desirable conditions.

Finally, the intern should gradually assume a full teaching schedule, step-by-step over a period of a year, starting with a very light teaching load. This would allow him to make adjustments and to work his way through the difficulties that beset a beginning teacher. As an intern, the individual would of course be paid a nominal salary. At the end of his period of internship he could be employed as a regular member of a school faculty.

The intern system should be directed and financed by state departments of education under general policies laid down by the profession.

Number of Training Complexes

The question of the number of complexes needed to produce an adequate supply of teachers is not easy to answer. It depends upon the demand for teachers and is related to the number of colleges and universities engaged in teacher education.

Where the population is sparse, as in the rural sections, a single complex may serve a large area covering a number of communities and school districts. In densely populated areas, as in the inner city, there may be one or more complexes for each district.

There are now approximately 900 higher institutions engaged in teacher education. Together they produce approximately 225,000 beginning teachers per year, or on the average about 250 teachers per institution. But the average productivity hides the great difference in teacher production among these schools. Indiana University turns out approximately 2,000 new teachers per year while Hendrix College produces about 30. This variation indicates that large universities or colleges may need to be involved in more than one complex to carry on their training programs, while a single complex may serve a number of small colleges and universities.

Limited experience with training centers seems to indicate that about 150 trainees is an optimum number per center. This estimate does not include teacher aides, part of whose training would be given in the complex. Considering teachers only, approximately 1,500 training centers in the entire country would be needed to keep up the present production of new teachers. But in order to produce the number of new teachers that the nation's schools require for quality education, the production of teachers must be raised to 384,000, or an increase of about 70 percent over the present output. To produce 384,000 teachers per year will require 2,500 training complexes. This figure is only a rough estimate, assuming that 150 trainees per complex is an optimum. Actually the number of trainees that can be adequately handled in a complex will depend upon the density of population, the number of available pupils, the amount of working space and equipment, and the size of the training staff.

Perhaps these centers should be considered as an initial step in the development of a bolder and more comprehensive organization of educational agencies into educational service districts.* The current links between the nation's more than 20,000 public school districts and its over 2,000 colleges (junior and senior) and universities are tenuous, usually far more apparent than real. Of course, there are examples of universities "adopting" individual schools with respect to teacher training and curriculum, and certain city-oriented or state universities accepting specific responsibilities with respect to planning and development for local and state government. But there exists no structured, hierarchical arrangements to link schools, higher education, and community (narrowly defined as a city or metropolitan area, broadly defined as parts of states or regions) and there is need for such new arrangements.

Educational systems, for some purposes, need to embrace areas that cut across city, county, and even state lines. Institutions of higher education can serve as the cores or nodes for such systems. These systems need not be organized as traditional geographical regions, that is, the boundaries need not be sharply defined lines—they can be zones. Or, if the boundaries are linear, then there can be overlapping of the new educational service districts. Moreover, the cores

---

* Educational service districts, as set forth here, were proposed by Saul B. Cohen, Graduate School, Clark University.

may be eccentric—i.e., higher education institutions may be located *outside* of the area which contains the schools and communities to be served.

The key to these new educational service districts may well be in the strategy of their design. In theory, we can look to approximately 2,100 such districts (to include 2,100 higher education institutions and an average of 10 school systems). One of the chief roles of such new districts would be in areas of teacher training and placement, paraprofessional recruitment and programming, curriculum innovation, design of a strategy for integrated schooling, and community social action programs (e.g., college student tutorial and peace corps-type activities, school programs for the disadvantaged, including boarding school and day care centers, and vocational education). The functions of these districts would also include research services to governmental agencies, training of social service personnel, law enforcement officers, and the like.

Criticisms and Replies

There will be many objections to the concept of the training complex. Aside from those that have to do with the details of operating and financing, there will be two objections that many critics will consider fundamental. The first is that the phasing out of student teaching eliminates the one aspect of teacher education that students now find most useful. Then, too, the jump from the training program to the work of the intern will be said to be too abrupt and will ensure failure for many students.

The first of these objections has already been answered in the argument in the preceding chapters. Student teaching is rated high by prospective teachers because it is the only work they have which resembles a training experience. Naturally when a program emphasizes formal courses which are not directly related to classroom work, the student will find that student teaching is relatively a more valuable experience. If the student were given a thorough program of training, the chances are that he would then value his training experience more highly than the formal courses.

The transition from the training program to the internship is no more of a problem than the transition from formal course work to student teaching. As a matter of fact, the transition will be much less a shock to the student because he will have been responsibly trained and will have had experience in handling classroom situations. The training program could mesh smoothly with an intern program so that the gap between the two would be practically eliminated.

A second objection is that the school situation will neutralize the intern's training. He will be required to conform to the mores of the school and the practices of his supervisor, and these might often be in conflict with the skills he acquired in training. The heart of this argument is that no matter how well an intern is trained he cannot hold out against the overwhelming climate of opinion the teachers and the school force upon him. In other words, it is argued that no improvement in teacher education can be effective until the schools themselves have been transformed. On the other hand, it is admitted that the schools cannot be made over without the improvement of teachers and without changes in the educational bureaucracy which, by its very nature, resists change. According to the argument, this is the predicament of teacher education.

There can be no question but that the forces which play upon a teacher at his job influence his attitudes and reactions toward pupils, parents, and his colleagues. He becomes captured by a network of activities and influences. In time, he becomes a guardian of this network and exhibits the protective behavior expected of one who favors the status quo. The individual is affected in this same way by any institutional system with which he becomes identified. Businessmen and industrialists are captured by their systems and medical doctors are shaped by the system of medical services. There is nothing new in this analysis. It has been pointed out time and again by social analysts as conservative as Sumner and as radical as Marx.

There are at least three attitudes one can take toward this fact of man's social existence. It can be argued that no system remains the same and that little by little any system will adjust to new circumstances. This rate of adjustment can be increased, according to this view, by deliberate efforts to change the system, first through study and research, and then through programs of action. Individuals who hold this view would point to Rice's description of thirty city school systems[2] in the 1890's and say that, in comparison, today's schools are far better than schools were then. They would point out that the practices for which schools are today criticized were the rule in the 1890's whereas today they are the exceptions. In reply some will say that even if the claim is true, it is irrelevant because today's demands upon the schools are so diversified and overwhelming that the gradual change the public depended upon for the improvement of its educational system in the first half of the century is no longer tolerable.

The second attitude is that of the aggressive activist who condemns the system as a whole and demands its complete reconstruction. To do this, goes the argument, the activist must be adept not only at persuasion but be backed by power groups who demand that the educational system be rebuilt. The influences within the new operating structure would shape teachers quite differently from the present system. If teacher training institutions were to identify themselves with these new power groups and move to reconstruct the educational system so as to build their programs of teacher preparation on this new educational base, their programs would be effective.

The critics of this view are quick to point out that what appears to be the wave of the future at one moment may later be dashed upon the rocks of resistance and dissipated. But perhaps their more cogent criticism is the claim that the establishment of a new system really leads nowhere. The forces within the new system influence individuals the same as in the old, so that the fossilization for which the old system was condemned is created anew. Furthermore, it is claimed that changes in a system do not change the behavior of individuals in any immediate and direct sense. The history of all radical social modifications, it is said, makes this extremely clear. So, in the end, the old habits and attitudes are taken over into the newer context. The change then boils down to the mere substitution of one set of power groups for another.

The third attitude toward the dilemma of teacher education takes a line of thought developed by sociologists and economists with respect to the nature of social systems and the ways in which they may be controlled.

A school is a system of interdependent variables. In this kind of system not everything has to be changed at once, and there is no particular factor that must be changed first. As Myrdal points out,[3] a change in any one variable affects all the others. The status of a minority group can be affected by changing any one of a number of factors: education, job opportunity, white prejudice, housing, and so on. So it is with a school system. A change in teachers' behavior will affect pupil conduct, achievement, and parental attitudes. Or a change in the attitudes of parents toward the school will modify the behavior of teachers and pupils. The question of which variables should be changed first comes down to the question of which among those accessible are most likely to have the greatest effect.

The phenomenon of change in an educational system entails what Myrdal referred to as the principle of cumulation.[4] If a school is not efficient, it will attract inefficient teachers and make them more inefficient. As a result, a vicious cycle is set in motion, progressively downgrading the school. This deterioration of the school is comparable to the tailspin in the economic system that we refer to as a depression. If the economy is left to itself without controls and if consumer demand declines, industry will reduce its production and increase unemployment. Unemployment will further depress consumer demands, leading to greater reduction in production and finally to economic collapse. But the reverse of the vicious cycle can also occur. In the economic system, if consumer demand increases, industry will expand its production. The industrial expansion will lead to further employment and to greater consumer demand. The result is an upswing in the economy in the direction of prosperity. So it is with the school. If well trained teachers are placed in a system, they will influence the atmosphere and practices of the school. This will lead to the selection of other teachers who are compatible with the new development. In this way the upward progress of the school is begun and can be maintained.

Some claim that the school system cannot be compared to the economic system or to the complex of attitudes and social practices that create and maintain the separation of the races within the nation. In this view, the economic system is not a set of relationships among individuals but such impersonal factors as capital, labor, goods and services, and fiscal policies of government. The techniques of manipulating and controlling these factors are quite different from the techniques of influencing and controlling the behavior of individuals, as in the school system.

This is all quite true, but, from the standpoint of the theory of social change assumed here, the difference is not crucial. The heart of the matter is the question of critical mass. In an interdependent system, the question is one of determining the amount of initial input necessary to initiate and sustain the chain reaction within the system. In the economic system, for example, experts can determine roughly the amount of governmental expenditure and the amount of tax reduction necessary to reverse the economy if it is tending toward a depression. A large amount of expenditure distributed over a considerable time span would make little difference in the regulation of the economy, whereas a large mass of money spent by the government in a short period of time would have a significant impact upon the total system. To change the educational system, it is necessary to determine the factors which would be effective in modifying the system and then to decide the amount of these factors necessary to initiate and sustain a chain reaction within the system.

The problem of changing instructional and administrative practices that go on within a school system is one of determining and producing the critical mass of personnel that will initiate the wave of change throughout the system itself. This critical mass can be produced by training complexes. The establishment of an appropriate number of these in an inner city, for instance, would lead to the production of enough interns and, through continuing education, enough career teachers to make a telling impact upon a school system within a short time. Furthermore, the complex would have sufficient community support to effect changes in the bureaucratic operation of the schools.

While the input of a critical mass of personnel is necessary, it is not sufficient. In addition, the program of training must be systematic and thorough. Anything significantly less than a year of full-time training would be wholly inadequate. The training can be given either in a fifth year, after the bachelor's degree, or earlier. But in both cases, the year of training should be unencumbered by other responsibilities.

Moreover, teachers who have gone through a program of intense training in the fundamentals outlined in the preceding chapters will not readily yield to the pressure of less competent teachers encountered on the job. Part of the failure of teacher education to influence the schools presumably arises from the fact that there has never been a program of teacher training, only a program of courses ending with student teaching. A teacher who completes such a program is in no position to stand his ground in a school system. But with a thorough program of training, there comes a commitment to do what the intern knows is appropriate. The commitment of an individual is not something he acquires simply by being told what to do. It comes from discipline in the ideas, procedures, and techniques by which a particular function is fulfilled.

CHAPTER 9

SUBJECT MATTER PREPARATION OF TEACHERS

To teach a child of suburbia, a teacher needs essentially the same subject matter as that required to teach a child of the slums. No matter what his social origin or environment, an individual must learn—and go on learning, at least minimally—how to get along in a technological, urbanized society, a society that requires scientific knowledge, social and political understanding, and a variety of skills and social techniques. Teachers of the affluent need no wider range of experience and knowledge than teachers of the poor. To specify the subject matter preparation of teachers of the disadvantaged is to indicate the preparation needed by all teachers.

The term "subject matter" is used in so many different senses, especially in pedagogical discourse, that some reference to its uses will help keep the discussion clear and consistent. The terms "subject matter" and "content" are ordinarily used interchangeably in pedagogical discourse. Sometimes the expression "knowledge" is used synonymously with these two terms. But if the term "knowledge" is used to designate information held to be true by a specific criterion such as the rules of empirical verification, then it is not always synonymous with "subject matter" or "content." Some subject matter does not satisfy any such criterion of acceptability. For example, a teacher may ask: "How would European society have changed had Hitler succeeded in his attempt to control Europe?" The question may stimulate the pupils' thinking and evoke extensive discussion. Much information, some true and some dubious, will be used in the discussion to defend answers and to argue against others. There can be no answer to the question that meets an acceptable criterion of validity. Nevertheless, we consider it the obligation of the teacher, by means of such questions, to open students' minds to those elements of subject matter which are considered to be intellectually fruitful. For this reason, we often equate knowledge, subject matter, and content.

In discourse on teacher preparation the expression "subject matter" ordinarily means the content of the disciplines offered in the curriculums of the universities and colleges. With certain qualifications which will be indicated later this is the basic sense in which the terms "subject matter," "content," and "knowledge" will be used in this chapter.

The problem of determining which content a teacher needs to know and what he needs to know about it is one that has not received the consideration it deserves. It would perhaps be useful if the content required for effective teaching were specified, but treatment of this is obviously impossible here. Instead, an attempt will be made to explore the general nature of the subject matter which a teacher needs and then set forth what the teacher needs to know about it.

Facets of Subject Matter Preparation

The subject matter preparation of the teacher has at least two facets. The first is the subject matter of the disciplines that make up his field of teaching. In some cases the teacher's field of instruction will be the same as a discipline. For instance, the field of a physics teacher is the same as the discipline of physics. In contrast, the instructional field of an English teacher may include such disciplines as literature, linguistics, rhetoric, and speech.

The teacher's knowledge of the disciplines that make up his field of instruction is, of course, ordinarily supplemented by knowledge of other disciplines. This additional work is sometimes referred to as general education and may be given in a number of forms: comprehensive courses, general studies, or specialized subjects.

The second facet of the subject matter that a teacher should have is that which is directly involved in teaching behavior. This is the knowledge that is taught to the pupil which he is expected to acquire. It is less than that contained in the disciplines of the teacher's field of instruction. The content of a discipline is unlimited and will expand as long as knowledge continues to accumulate. In contrast, the content of subjects of instruction must always be accommodated to factors such as time, capacity, and prior learning.

Besides knowledge in these two senses, the teacher should also possess knowledge about knowledge.[1] This need is not obvious, and the teacher seldom recognizes it himself, being immersed in the subject matter he is teaching as well as absorbed in his interaction with pupils. The instructional subject matter influences the teacher's behavior. He verbalizes its elements, relates them to one another and to the experiences of his pupils. He asks questions and responds to pupil answers in terms of his command of the content. So, the teacher is seldom aware of his need to climb out of the subject matter and take a broad, objective look at what he is doing and at his difficulties in handling the content. To climb out of and over the subject matter, to look at it from the outside, is to increase control over teaching behavior and the clarity and thoroughness of presentation.

Knowledge about knowledge in general enables the teacher to gain this higher and more comprehensive perspective. This sort of knowledge is built upon more particular knowledge of the elements of subject matter and the relations among them, the uses of the disciplines' knowledge, and the ways their information is manipulated and its dependability decided.

To sum up, the subject matter preparation of the teacher should consist of two interrelated parts: first, command of the content of the disciplines constituting his teaching field and of the subject matter to be taught; and second, command of knowledge about knowledge. This chapter is devoted to an exploration of the first of these two components of the teacher's preparation.

Nature of the Disciplines

A discipline is an area of inquiry containing a distinctive body of concepts and principles, with techniques for exploring the area and for correcting and expanding the body of knowledge.[2] The above is perhaps the most commonly used definition and the one used in the present discussion. A discipline may begin with inquiry into practical problems, but it does not depend upon investigation of such problems for its development. Classical physics, for instance, may have begun with the practical problems of navigation, projectile paths, and air pressure in mines. But ties with these problems were often cut and much of the subsequent development of physics resulted from its inner dynamics. So many, or most, of the problems arise within a discipline itself. Sometimes they are rooted in contradictions that emerge among basic concepts and presuppositions. Solutions to these basic problems bring revolutionary changes in the discipline, as the transition from classical to modern physics. But more often the growth of a discipline is attributable to work on problems of lesser scope and of little theoretical interest.

Though often confused, a field is distinct, we may agree, from a discipline. A field may be made up of content from several disciplines. The field of education, for instance, contains content borrowed from the disciplines of psychology, sociology, history, and philosophy. A field serves a social function; it is oriented to practical concerns. The function of the field of civil engineering is to design and construct public and private works; that of law is to serve justice. By contrast, to continue our past distinction, a discipline is committed to no extrinsic end. There is certainly no external criterion by which its method and content are to be judged.

A discipline is not to be confused with subjects of instruction.[3] No set of subjects can exhaust a discipline, although they typically contain its fundamentals. A discipline is infinite. But subjects of instruction are limited by the purposes for which they are developed.

Preparation in the Disciplines

Preparation of the teacher in the disciplines is bound up in the problem of providing a general education for every student regardless of his future occupation. General education assumes that there is a body of concepts, principles, and skills that everyone should possess or know about because of its usefulness for all persons by virtue of their common role in society. This aspect of the teacher's preparation should be no more a concern of those responsible for teacher education than of those who are interested in the preparation of lawyers, doctors, journalists, political scientists, or laymen.

A teacher's advanced preparation in a discipline cannot be essentially different from that of students who wish to prepare themselves for research careers, or to pursue a special interest, or simply to deepen their knowledge. Courses designed to provide advanced work in a discipline can be modified only to a limited degree in the direction of being "service courses." Their content is mainly the concepts, principles, and skills essential to the student's further learning in the discipline, arranged in order of increasing complexity. Efforts to adapt the content to outside criteria, such as the demands of a profession, have been thwarted at the practical level by the demands of the discipline for order and rigor.

Comprehensive courses in programs of general education have sometimes been made up of content from various aspects of a single discipline, as is the case in general biology. Where such courses have involved more than one discipline, as in courses in contemporary civilization where materials from art, science, economics, and politics are used, the principles of unification are usually temporal sequence and interdependence among the elements of culture. If these courses survive, and they often do not, their survival can be attributed largely to this tendency to rely on the discipline of history. Any demand for courses prepared especially for teachers runs against the experience of the last fifty years and disregards the nature of the disciplines. The content of a course can hardly be selected and ordered by extrinsic criteria, such as the needs of a profession, without violating the characteristic way of thinking of the discipline.

We do not mean that courses in the disciplines should not be criticized or reformed. Obviously courses change in both content and structure in response to criticisms and developments in the disciplines, and many of these will be provoked by *outside* developments. But the changes will probably always be consistent with the discipline. Nor is it to be understood that knowledge contained in the disciplines cannot be lifted out and organized for other purposes. Knowledge can be and is used, independent of the disciplines, and often in non-academic circles. But even in academic programs knowledge can be selected from various disciplines, then organized and taught in relation to a wide range of human concerns. The interdisciplinary approach to curriculum development is based on this fact. But this type of program should not be confused with a program to prepare the student in the disciplines.

In the development of a program to prepare teachers in the disciplines, the primary problem is deciding which courses are most clearly related to the various teaching fields. There have been two main approaches to this problem. One was the development of separate curriculums for the various fields of teaching. This has often been done by committees whose members are chosen from the faculties of the subject matter departments and the relevant pedagogical departments. The curriculum is planned to satisfy a major in a discipline so that the student may advance to graduate study in the discipline. Certain courses are included because they are needed by a teacher. For example, an English curriculum for the high school teacher may include courses in speech correction, linguistics, and the sociology of language, along with the conventional courses in rhetoric and literature.

This way of planning the curriculum of the high school teacher provides him with a wider range of information than if he is expected to satisfy only the requirements of majors and minors. The English teacher, for example, who has some understanding of the sociology of language, speech correction, or linguistics is better prepared to handle high school English than a teacher who has a straight major in the field of English with concentration in literature. He may also take work in other disciplines more advanced than that which a major in English ordinarily elects.

The second solution to the problem of providing preparation in the disciplines was to require two years of general education, capped by two years of specialized work. The program of general education consisted of comprehensive or general courses, organized within a discipline, and sometimes including aspects of related disciplines. These courses purported to give an overall view of the academic terrain, to organize the specialized but related elements of the intellectual culture so that they gave significance to the multiplicity of institutions and activities that comprise society. But the specialized work continued to be the conventional courses in various disciplines.

Criticisms of
Discipline-Oriented Programs

These two approaches have been criticized on the grounds that they lead to fragmented programs and that their relevance to man's basic questions is at best tenuous. Several years ago, before the knowledge explosion had been reflected in the curriculums of the universities, Hocking pointed out that the Harvard University catalog contained over 1,200 courses, and that a student could hope to take only a few of them.[4] If it is assumed that 120 credit hours are required for a bachelor's degree and that each course is a three-hour course, the student would take a total of forty courses in his college career. Forty courses out of 1,200 is not impressive. The student would have only a fragment of knowledge. Even if he took a considerable proportion of those forty courses in a particular discipline, or even in comprehensive courses, his knowledge would still be extremely limited. Fragmented programs of instruction have increased with the knowledge explosion so that the picture Hocking drew of Harvard in the 1940's is now much enlarged and is true of nearly every institution in the country.

The movement to develop programs of general education in the first half of this century was an attempt to grapple with the problem of fragmentation. This movement toward integration is but one aspect of man's perennial quest for unity for the sake of better understanding. He has sought it in substance and in method. In nature he has looked for some simple element from which everything else is derived, as did Democritus, who said that the real world consists of atoms qualitatively alike but different in shape. But once the atom had been established as an entity, it turned out that atoms were not as similar as had been supposed and the quest continued. In turn, the atom itself fell apart and substantive unity eluded him again. An educational counterpart of this search for substantive unity is found in the belief that there must be some elements of knowledge so fundamental that they include all others. This belief has been eroded by the acids of specialized knowledge. But there is still the belief that in a given field there are basic ideas that unify content.[5] Of course, some ideas are more fundamental than others in the sense that they include others. They therefore have greater explanatory power, and, other things being equal, are more valuable educationally. But it is questionable whether there are enough of these ideas of greater generality to underwrite a program of general education.

Those who have given up the search for unity in substance have turned to intellectual method. They believe that there is a common way by which all knowledge is established. This is the method of intelligence by which the individual moves from a perplexing situation to a resolution of it. The pattern of the method is closely associated with Dewey's analysis of thinking[6] and is foreshadowed, according to its proponents, in the behavior of lower forms of life. All questions, from those of fact to those of value and worth, are to be settled by the same intellectual procedure.

Given a common intellectual method, it is possible to find unity despite the great diversity of content. This unity is found in the intellectual method rather than in the subject matter. So, it was possible to have a great diversity of specialized courses and still maintain a stable integration as long as all were disciplined in the same method. This position was sloganized as "Don't teach *what*, but *how* to think." But the doctrine of universal method, like that of substantive unity, has come under attack in recent years. There is much less confidence in its validity now than there was three decades ago. Questions about what is most worthwhile, good, or beautiful do not seem to yield to the same method as questions about "what" or "how." Furthermore, each discipline appears to have its own particular mode of investigation. Proof in mathematics is not the same thing as proof in history; truth in *Hamlet* or *Cry the Beloved Country* is not the same as truth in Newton's *Principia*. Again and again there are disparate methods in the same disciplines. The genetic method of inquiry in psychology is different from experimental and statistical methods in that discipline. Yet in all these there are similarities as well as differences. But they can be found only at high levels of abstraction where they have no use or else no rigor. Whatever elements of method the disciplines have in common are so abstract and formal that they have little importance as unifying principles.

These efforts to create a program of education to preserve man's prudence and general perspective did little to restore the unity of outlook and feeling of control over his destiny that man once gained from his pursuit of knowledge in the classic liberal arts. The demise of general education seems to indicate that the observation of Barzun that "the liberal arts tradition is dead or dying" may indeed be so.

But the search for a general perspective can be surrendered only at the risk of social disaster in a free society. The paradox of our times is this—at the very moment when specialized knowledge and specialized activities are molding men with fragmentary minds and narrow perspectives, man is called upon to see the world as a whole, to see the interdependence of its parts, and to have the insight and prudence to deal with it constructively.

To provide a program of education that will enable each man to put the parts of his culture together, to see the interdependence of its many social functions, and to have the patience and wisdom to remedy the dysfunctions that occur, is the task of those who are concerned with general education. An educational program that would lead to such results should be the basic education of a teacher.

There is no ready solution to this paradox. One of the current approaches is to emphasize the role of the disciplines in the education of the individual. The two elements of a discipline that are of special importance are the system of concepts that constitutes its body of knowledge and the techniques by which its knowledge is corrected and expanded. A program of general education would then consist of the concepts and techniques of a few basic areas of inquiry.

The phenomena dealt with in a discipline are interpreted and understood in terms of concepts. The order of these concepts and their interrelations supply whatever unity a discipline has. As far as it goes, this answer to the paradox seems to have considerable merit. It would lift the educational program out of the domain of mere fact and would go a long way toward reducing the fragmentation that occurs from specialized courses that deal with small pieces of reality. It would also provide training in some of the intellectual processes which are the basis of man's rationality.

However, this approach suffers from two defects. The first is that it provides for no integration among the disciplines themselves. This would seem to be possible only if there are concepts of such great generality that they embrace the basic ideas of two or more disciplines. As already pointed out, it is doubtful that enough of these concepts exist to give unity to any sizable portion of the curriculum. But when education is being called on to build a common perspective, as it is today, the investigation deserves renewed effort.

Perhaps a more telling criticism argues that emphasis upon conceptual content and methods of the disciplines is no guarantee that the basic questions that concern man will be confronted. What is the purpose of man's struggle on earth? Why should anyone attempt to find his niche in a bureaucratic society and prepare himself to make good in it? Why attempt to follow the established social and political procedures when they do not seem to lead to the goals which are promised? What is the point of trying to make good in a world that seems bent upon self-destruction? These are the kinds of questions modern man is concerned about and they are precisely the kinds of questions which most, if not all, the disciplines seem to neglect. Perhaps it is not the lack of some all-embracing unity that impoverishes the educational program. Perhaps it is the failure of discipline-oriented education to confront with intellectual refinement and integrity the basic value issues of the modern world. The absence of this concern in the curriculum of the colleges and universities perhaps explains the revolt of students against the education they receive.

Inclusion of fundamental value questions in a discipline-oriented program of education may be more difficult than appears on the surface. The disciplines, as previously observed, have their own inherent problems and logic. Physics deals with the problems of physics and not the problems of man. Only by implication is it relevant to man's present-day concerns. So it is with most other disciplines. The basic value questions that haunt a growing number of youths and their elders are extrinsic to the disciplines and can be included in them only by distorting their character. When the humanities are treated as disciplines, as is increasingly the case, they too become separated from man's newest uncertainties and apprehensions. Philosophy, for instance, becomes less concerned with man's problems and more concerned with problems of philosophy as it takes on the character of a rigorous discipline.

Preparation in the
Content of Instruction

Today, the preparation of a teacher begins with the subject matter of one or more disciplines. The prospective teacher takes introductory courses, then more advanced work in a discipline, so that the knowledge in his mind becomes an organized subject. His studies have prepared him to think as a specialist.

If the subject matter the teacher is to teach and the principles of its organization were the same as in college courses in the disciplines, this program would perhaps be sufficient. Except for the vocational fields, the basic content of the school program is drawn from the disciplines. But what is and should be taught in elementary and secondary schools, and how it should be arranged for instruction, cannot be equated with the content and its arrangement in discipline-oriented courses.

A great deal of what the prospective teacher learns from his study of the disciplines is not to be taught to children and youths. It functions in the teacher's mind as marginal knowledge, not as instructional content. Also, the subject matter actually taught to pupils is not always the same as that contained in the courses of the disciplines. Much of the subject matter taught by the elementary teacher has been virtually ignored by the academic departments of colleges and universities. The elementary teacher may take work in a number of disciplines, but still learn very little about some of the content he is to teach. Until quite recently, the elementary teacher could find no work in mathematics that prepared him to teach arithmetic. Neither could he find much in college literature useful in developing a reading program. This situation still exists in most higher institutions.

Much of the content taught by the elementary teacher was acquired by him in the public school and from courses on teaching the various subjects. For example, a pedagogical course in elementary science will not only deal with ways of teaching science but with the content to be taught. The prospective teacher studies the facts and principles of science that he will teach to elementary pupils and does some experiments which he can do in his classroom. Some of the content and experiments taught in this course may be covered at a sophisticated level in the departments of science, but the work will be so far removed from the experiences of elementary pupils that it is necessary to change the content to a simpler form. The same observations could be made about work in reading, social studies, art, and other subjects taught in the schools. The National Science Foundation has funded special projects to develop elementary science, but there is virtually nothing similar for other subjects.

Perhaps the failure of academic departments to assume more responsibility for the subject matter preparation of the elementary teacher can also be attributed to the fact that the elementary school has not been perceived as affecting the quality of students admitted to academic departments. High school work has been looked upon as preparatory to the work in these departments. So the academic faculties have set their priorities on influencing the preparation of teachers for the secondary schools.

Furthermore, the content of the elementary school, being more unlike that of the college departments, has been more of a mystery to the academic faculties. They have not known how to fit the broad preparation of the elementary teacher into a system of majors and minors and other requirements for a liberal arts degree. Recently academic faculties have pressed for specialization in the elementary school like that in high schools and colleges, and for more specialized subject matter preparation of the teacher. This answer to the question of the teacher's preparation is filled with pedagogical problems and assumes at bottom that what is good for the academic specialist is good for the elementary pupil and teacher.

Perhaps the basic reason academic departments have not designed courses for elementary school teachers is that they might have to construct non-discipline-oriented courses. The subject matter could not simply be selected by the criterion of what content will advance the prospective teacher in the discipline.

The high school curriculum is much more like the discipline-oriented courses of the college. But even here it is necessary that the prospective teacher give special consideration to the content he will actually teach. He must not assume that pupils have the same mental set and motivation as the specialist in a discipline. Of course some pupils will pursue knowledge just for the thrill of learning, but the great majority will do so only occasionally, for the orientation of children and youths is to the activities around them. They do not ordinarily think in terms of history, mathematics, psychology, economics, and other disciplines. And efforts to make them do so will not often succeed.

For this reason it is necessary that the prospective teacher rethink much of the content of the disciplines as it relates to the life of the pupil. The concern of youths in suburbia with major problems in their daily lives and with society has been documented in a number of studies. In one of the subsidiary reports of the National Advisory Commission on Civil Disorders the same concern is reported among the youths of the ghettos.[7] From a sample of teachers in fifteen major cities of the country, it was found that forty-three percent of these teachers thought that the concerns of students extended beyond what the program of the school dealt with. When this forty-three percent were asked to indicate what these other concerns were, they mentioned serious problems more often than frivolous matters. Sixty-three percent of these teachers felt that the students were concerned with basic problems of society, questions of their own futures, and everyday problems such as relations with their parents. Yet the academic program of the teacher typically ignores these matters. The teacher is usually unprepared to deal with these problems. He has neither the relevant knowledge nor the skills to find and organize the subject matter for problematic study. Because he lacks specific preparation, a teacher may seek to avoid these concerns of youths whenever possible.

To handle these problems the teacher needs modules of knowledge. Discipline-oriented courses are not designed at present to provide them. The courses cover too much, require too much time, and are not focused on the concerns of youths. Treatment of the tax structure at the high school level, for instance, does not require the background of a course in taxation though it may gain from some knowledge of the fruitful questions which emerge among specialists.

Seminars in which these problems are studied should be instituted for both elementary and high school teachers-in-training. The materials of these seminars should be selected from whatever disciplines are relevant. The mode of study should be that of problem solving and the prospective teachers themselves should assume a large share of the responsibility for analyzing the problems, selecting and organizing the materials, and carrying on discussion. By taking on this responsibility, they would learn to think through problems on their own and would acquire some of the skills essential to the identification and location of relevant materials. They would also experience the kinds of difficulties their own pupils will encounter when they work on problems of their own and will be better able to deal with them. Furthermore, the teacher-to-be will gain from these experiences a greater facility in the indispensable skill of handling ideas in discussion.

To be prepared in the subject matter of instruction is to know the content to be taught and how the content can be related to the interest and experience of children and youths. To prepare the teacher in this subject matter will require courses oriented to the teacher's need for knowledge that can be tied in with the life of children and youths rather than discipline-oriented courses.[8]

To go from the disciplines to the content of instruction involves a tremendous burden of translation. A teacher must sift out what is directly relevant to his work even for the purposes of his own interpretive background. Only in part can the content of the disciplines be adapted to the child's level of knowledge and experience. The difficulties teachers have with the disadvantaged pupil arise partly because the two levels of cultural existence are so far apart. The chasm between the sophisticated and abstract subject matter of the college course and the concrete and simple world of younger children is so wide that teachers find it extremely difficult to negotiate. For many a teacher of the disadvantaged child, bridging this gap is almost impossible.

To sum up, the teacher should know the content he is to teach as well as that of the disciplines from which his instructional subject matter may be taken. The first is necessary for teaching anything at all. The second supplies a depth of knowledge essential to the teacher's feeling of intellectual security and his ability to handle instructional content with greater understanding.

Need for Cooperative Planning

The failure of academic faculties to realize that what they teach in the discipline-oriented courses is not the complete subject matter preparation of the teacher is one obstacle to the development of a more adequate program. Another obstacle is the failure of the pedagogical faculties to define their own role in the teacher's subject matter preparation. Perhaps the most serious result of these failures is the inadequate preparation of the teacher in the subject matter which he will actually teach. Often he cannot follow its roots very far into the disciplines or handle it skillfully in teaching. And he is frequently unable to see its significance in the life of his pupils. This situation is due to the fact that courses in the content of instruction have been taught either by academic instructors who have little knowledge of children, youths, and the curriculum of the public school, or by members of pedagogical departments who may know a great deal about children but little about the disciplines.

To develop a program of subject matter preparation for teachers it is necessary to have cooperative planning that involves academic departments, pedagogical departments, and the schools. But such joint planning can be successful only if the parties involved clearly understand the role of the disciplines and their limitations in the preparation of the teacher, the role of the pedagogical departments, and the function of the teaching profession (discussed later) in the shaping of programs for the preparation of teachers.

The subject matter preparation of teachers is too complex, too embedded in the disciplines and in the demands of the public for a meaningful education to be left in the hands of either the academic or pedagogical departments alone. And it is so closely identified with the needs of the professional teachers that they should not be ignored in the planning.

CHAPTER 10

PREPARATION IN KNOWLEDGE *ABOUT* SUBJECT MATTER

The control of the teacher's own behavior is one of the main outcomes of an adequate program of teacher preparation. Those responsible for designing programs of teacher education must determine the knowledge appropriate to such control. It has long been recognized that the teacher's knowledge of his subject matter has a controlling influence on what he does in the classroom. If he is teaching mathematics, his behavior will be different from his behavior in teaching literature. He may perform the operations involved in mathematical proof or show how to solve a particular type of problem in arithmetic. If he is teaching literature to elementary pupils, he may read part of a story to enlist pupil interest or invite pupils to recount a story they have read. At the high school level he may explore the imagery of a literary passage. There can be little doubt that the nature of the subject matter has as much influence upon the behavior of the teacher as his knowledge of the pupils.

The teacher's psychological knowledge, discussed in an earlier chapter, also influences his attitudes towards pupils and shapes in some degree how he will deal with the pupils and the content of instruction.

It has only recently been recognized that there is another sort of knowledge that can influence the performance of the teacher: that used in thinking about the subject matter and the logical operations used in manipulating it. It can be said, for instance, that a statement made in a biology class is not true, that a definition given in a physics class is incorrect, or that there is ethnic bias in a particular passage. These assertions are ways of talking about the subject matter, and the knowledge used in making such claims is what is meant here by knowledge *about* subject matter.

Ways of Talking About Subject Matter

There are at least five ways of talking about the subject matter of a teaching field. The first is to discuss its elements. An item of content can be referred to as a generalization, a value, etc. The second way is to discuss the logic of the content. We can refer to a given bit of subject matter as an explanation or another as a justification. The third is to discuss the uses of the subject matter. These are the generic ways in which knowledge functions regardless of the concerns and problems of the one who possesses it. The fourth is to point out social biases in the content. The fifth is to consider the relevance of the subject matter to the present and future needs of pupils. The purpose here is to explore these five ways of talking about subject matter.

To be able to talk about the content of instruction is to climb above it and to analyze it from this higher and more inclusive perspective. To do that requires an appropriate level of language and one that the teacher is able to converse in. It is impossible to say anything about subject matter using the vocabulary of the subject matter itself. For example, we cannot say anything about sentences or the words contained in them without the terminology of grammar; we cannot say that this word is a noun and that one a verb without the terms "noun" and "verb," which are not words in the sentence. Similarly, the teacher must have command of the language and the knowledge used to talk about the subject matter of his field of teaching.

The teacher who possesses this sort of knowledge and language has an extra dimension from which to observe his own teaching behavior as well as that of his pupils. A person who has command of the knowledge and language of grammar is able to look at his own linguistic behavior in a way quite different from one who can express himself in words but knows nothing about language itself. A person who knows grammar is able to monitor his linguistic behavior while making appropriate changes in it for better communication.

So it is with teaching behavior. To handle the subject matter of instruction in certain difficult situations the teacher does well to understand its elements, its logical dimensions, its uses, its relation to pupil needs, and the degree of its social "neutrality." Because teachers do not now possess such understanding, they frequently handle the subject matter of instruction in superficial ways. Consequently, class discussion often suffers from undue vagueness and ambiguity, from unfounded and unchallenged claims, from a failure to develop the significance of the content.

Knowledge About Forms of Subject Matter

The subject matter of each field of teaching is a mixture of different forms of knowledge. All of the fields contain concepts. Some contain laws or law-like statements. Others contain rules and theorems. And still others include values either as major emphases or as incidental to other forms of content. It is important for the teacher to be aware of these knowledge forms because studies have shown that each is taught and learned in a different way. Current programs of subject matter preparation do not enable a teacher to identify the forms of subject matter or to relate teaching behavior appropriately to the ways they are most easily learned. In one study of the sensitivity of teachers to these elements of knowledge, the transcribed classroom discourse of some twenty high school teachers was given to them and each was asked to identify the places where he was dealing with concepts, values, and facts. The ability of the teachers to identify these places was not any greater than would be expected of individuals of comparable education who had not been trained to teach.[1]

A teacher who is unable to stand off and look at his subject matter, or view the classroom discussion and say now we are dealing with a concept and now we are dealing with a law—or now with a story and now with an explanation— simply cannot have adequate control over the processes of instruction. Faculties in the various disciplines have failed to analyze the content of instruction into its logically and pedagogically significant elements. Teachers who are ignorant of these elements do not know how to handle their content, other than by common sense. A teacher cannot handle with skill a form of knowledge he cannot identify and whose structure he does not know.

Another way to talk about the forms of subject matter is to refer to the different types of statements made in class or contained in text materials.[2] Here are but a few illustrations of these different types. First, definitions: this is a type of content that gives rules for using words. "Para-rubber is a native rubber from a South American tree of the spurge family" is a sentence which tells how the expression "para-rubber" is to be used. Any time the expression "native rubber from a South American tree of the spurge family" is used, the word "para-rubber" can be substituted for it, and vice versa. There is a common referent of the word "para-rubber" and its defining expression. But in other definitions there need be no referent at all, as in some mathematical terms.

Definitions are sometimes confused with statements of fact. A biology teacher said to his class that there were very few thorough-bred race horses in the United States. Some of his pupils replied that their parents told them that there are a *large* number of thoroughbred race horses. The teacher then observed that perhaps they were not using the expression "thoroughbred" in the same sense and asked them to come prepared the next day with definitions of the term taken from encyclopedias or dictionaries. Next day there were at least four definitions given by members of the class. The teacher wrote them all on the blackboard, but after that he was at a loss to know what to do with them. There were claims and counter-claims as to which one was to be accepted.

In the discussion that followed the teacher did not know the meaning of the term "definition" and hence got into all sorts of difficulty. For one thing, one of the pupils insisted that *his* definition was true and that all the others were false: "A thoroughbred race horse is a flat race horse originating in England," he said. After some discussion, an observer in the room asked if the following would be acceptable: "a flat race horse originating in England we choose to call a thoroughbred." The pupil replied, "No. You do not *choose* to call him a thoroughbred. That is what he is." This bit of discussion clearly indicated confusion in the pupil's mind. He was assuming that a set of words was the state of affairs. This is an assumption that particularly needs to be set straight when the class discussion is concerned with ethnic biases. The discussion proceeded on the assumption that these definitions were statements of fact. As long as the discussion was based on this assumption, there was no way of resolving the issue before the class. For definitions are conventions and they are fruitful or not fruitful, convenient or not convenient. They are not "true" in the same sense in which a statement such as "Cats scratch" can be said to be true.

Another type of content is one which commends or criticizes, approves or disapproves. It expresses a rating of an object or event. These are referred to as value statements. "*A Tale of Two Cities* is a good novel," "An overemphasis on nationalism is bad," "X is a good mechanic" are all statements of value. It is often believed that statements of this type express only attitudes. So when the teacher does identify a value judgment, he is apt to treat it as a mere statement of opinion, especially if it conflicts with other judgments made by either the teacher or members of the class. In these cases, there is no examination made into the grounds for judgment, and yet such examination is often fruitful. The examination of value statements can lead to a search for criteria by which objects and events are judged to be of value, and for evidence matching the criteria. This can be a very valuable intellectual undertaking in a schoolroom. But all too often the teacher does not recognize value statements as such, or else does not know how to deal with them when he is aware of them.

In addition, the teacher and his pupils are constantly using empirical subject matter: this kind of content is about the sensible world. The truth of these sentences is determined by observations:

"The barometer reading is 29.3," "Galileo died in 1642," "A confined volume of gas will vary inversely with the pressure if the temperature is held constant." These are all examples of empirical statements, the truth of which can be determined by specifiable tests.

This content is easily confused with the other types mentioned above, as well as with analytic content which is very often in the same context. For instance, the analytic statement that "Anything which is a material body occupies space" can be easily confused with an empirical one. But a little analysis will reveal that when it is said, "Anything which is a material body occupies space," no information is given that is not already known when something is said to be a material body. For the meaning of the expression "occupies space" is already included in the meaning of the expression "material body." To think of a material body is to think of something in space.

There are many other types of content used in classroom discourse. Among these are particulars, as when one says, "This rod is three feet long." Some content consists of generalizations for which there are instances, as "All presidents of the United States have been males." Some generalizations, the more powerful ones, have no instances. In the case of the law of gravity, we cannot point to instances but only to the rise and fall of tides and other phenomena which are associated with the law by a chain of inferences. Then there is prescriptive content which gives us directions as to how something is to be done. Prescriptions usually take the form of rules, and there are several different types of rules. Then there are counter-factuals which state what might have occurred had a certain state of affairs existed. For example, if the American Civil War had not occurred, the institution of slavery might still be in existence in the United States. The teacher needs to understand the nature and limitations of all these types of content if he is to control his behavior and that of his pupils and have a greater degree of insight into his subject matter.

Logical Aspects of Subject Matter

Each field of instruction not only contains forms of knowledge such as definitions and cause-effect relationships, but also involves logical activities such as defining, explaining, and justifying.[3] The teacher should be thoroughly trained in the performance of such operations, as well as in the structural analysis of them. To understand their logical structure is to treat the subject matter with greater clarity and thoroughness. For example, high school history teachers often use law-like statements without recognizing that they do so. These are statements that have the form of a cause-effect relationship, but have not been empirically tested and established.

Suppose that a teacher is discussing the migration of Europeans to the New World and asks why the Pilgrims came. A pupil says that they came because they wanted a place where they could worship as they pleased. Implicit in this verbal exchange is a law-like proposition. It may be stated as follows: If persons of such and such characteristics are denied the right to worship according to their beliefs, and if there is free territory into which they can move and worship, then they will move into the new region. This statement gives a set of conditions from which, by hypothesis, a set of consequences follows. It is a general statement that covers all human beings who satisfy the given conditions.

The pupils implicitly suppose that the Pilgrims were persons possessing certain characteristics and were denied the right to worship as they pleased. They assumed further that the Pilgrims were aware of America as a territory into which they could move and worship. The teacher and the pupils thus implicitly treated the Pilgrims as a particular case covered by the general principle.

The epistemology of history is a controversial subject, and many historians would deny that this is a fruitful way to deal with historical questions. This is not an issue here. The point is not whether teachers should use law-like statements as they teach history, but that they should not do so unwittingly as they do now.

A teacher who fails to analyze implicit law-like statements, typically assumed in instruction, is laying the groundwork for loose thinking by his pupils. It is through understanding and analyzing the logical operations that the teacher comes to understand the logical structure of his subject matter and handle it adequately in the course of teaching.

It should be clear from what has been said that the methods of problem solving are not the only cognitive processes that a teacher should understand. The teacher should also know the structure of such logical operations as classifying, explaining, defining, rating, and justifying, in addition to those discussed above.

Knowledge About Relevance and Uses of Subject Matter

The teacher is constantly asked: "Why should I learn that?" "What is the use of studying history?" "Why should I be required to take biology?" If the intent of these questions is to ask what use can one make of them in everyday activities, only general answers are possible. We can and do talk about the relevance of subject matter to the decisions and activities that pupils will have to make.[4] We know, among other things, that they must:

—choose and follow a vocation,
—exercise the tasks of citizenship,
—engage in personal relationships,
—take part in culture-carrying activities.

In this context of general necessities teachers must learn to assess the content of the educational program. But their judgment will always be clouded by the vicissitudes of life and the lack of a one-to-one correspondence between most school learnings and life activities. It can be argued with some justification that anything that one learns is used, even if very indirectly. So the question of relevance boils down to the question of what is most assuredly useful. Some of the things which are learned seem to function directly, and their use can be easily seen. For example, the use of handwriting is so obvious that few, if any, pupils ever ask a question about it. The same thing can be said about the basic operations in arithmetic and about the ability to read. In fact, the closer learning comes to being identified with skills that are used in everyday activities the fewer questions will be asked about its utility.

As the subject matter of instruction moves away from the fundamental skills and into abstract content, the pupil is apt to become more concerned about the usefulness of the content he is studying. Unfortunately, the utility of this form of subject matter is much more difficult to demonstrate, and pupils may have the feeling that, after all, it is not worth a great deal. But the tendency of the schools to lose contact with the life of the people, as social change becomes ever more rapid, points to the urgent necessity of continuing the efforts to keep school as close to life as possible.

While there may be no definitive answer to the pupils' concern about the utility of abstract subject matter, it is valuable for the teacher to understand the ways in which such content is used. These explanations will, of course, not allay the suspicions of some students but they will be useful to the teacher in relating the content of instruction to the lives of his students.

Perhaps the chief reason utility of abstract knowledge cannot be demonstrated to the skeptic is that a great deal of it functions as a second-order utility. A first-order utility is illustrated in the skills that we use directly in everyday behavior such as handwriting and reading. The second-order utility consists of a learning that shapes behavior, but which is not, itself, directly observable in behavior. For example, a person may believe that all individuals are of equal worth as human beings. But the behavior which he exhibits toward individuals may be traceable to it only through a chain of inferences from the belief to the behavior. These uses of knowledge that are not directly observable in behavior may be classified into three categories: associative, interpretive, and applicative.[5]

The associative use of knowledge involves psychological relationships among ideas. One hears the word "hedge apple" and thinks of the contours of the brain, or sees red shoes and thinks of the Chinese communists: there is no logical relation in these associations. They result from putting things together that do not ordinarily go together. The practical value of this use of knowledge is not immediately evident. Nevertheless, there is reason to suspect that a great deal of what is called creativity and originality results from this tendency of the human mind to make free associations.

The second way in which knowledge is used is in the interpretation of objects and events. Perhaps the most fundamental aspect of an individual's thinking is the way he divides up the elements of his environment. As pointed out earlier, man understands his environment by classifying its various aspects. The categories into which his environment is classified constitute his conceptual system. So, the objects and events with which the individual deals have meaning in terms of the way in which they fit into this system of ideas. In short, the individual responds to anything in his environment in terms of how he interprets it.

In an earlier time an individual who committed some heinous act was considered to be a tool of the devil. He was interpreted as being an evil person. As such, he was punished for his crime by doing penance or forfeiting his life. Today such behavior is frequently taken to indicate that he is mentally ill. When he is interpreted as suffering from an illness, he may then be treated as a sick person and hospitalized. So the concepts and general principles that an individual has acquired shape his understanding of what goes on about him and influence his behavior. This is one of the reasons a teacher should give considerable care to the selection of concepts to be taught and to the ways of teaching them. But he may find it difficult to explain to pupils how this conceptual knowledge will be used in their daily lives.

Some of the knowledge which we have is used in solving problems. Such knowledge forms as concepts, general principles, and particular statements of fact are used in working out ways of dealing with new situations. The application of knowledge to new circumstances is, of course, not simply a matter of recalling it. Rather it is the association of knowledge in such a way that new insights emerge. Usually the applicative use is facilitated by resorting to analogies: the new situation is compared to one which is already known and for which a solution has been worked out. But the process is not as mechanical as one might think, for, as Dewey said many years ago, a solution to a new situation often just seems to happen. It pops into our mind and we are at a loss to account for it.

These three categories of utility are to be found in the thinking of all individuals, no matter what their occupation, social position, or social origins. In a free society they function not only in one's occupational life but also in the communal life where a consensus must be built through the arts of reflection and persuasion to support public policies and decisions. It is extremely important for teachers to know these uses of subject matter and sensitize their pupils to them.

Sensitivity to Biases of Subject Matter

Another aspect of the teacher's preparation is his awareness of the racial and social biases the materials of instruction may reflect. Absolute objectivity is not possible. As Darwin pointed out long ago, even the selection of facts is always for or against some idea. Nevertheless biases that deprecate anyone's genetic inheritance or attribute inferiority to any group are to be tracked down and eliminated, as far as possible. However, a distinction should be made between materials prepared for instruction, and literary and other artistic works. The glories of man as well as his frailties and foibles are depicted in works of art. There man can see himself reflected as in a mirror and to some measure can become aware of what he is. This heritage of man's account of himself is to be preserved intact even though in its encyclopedic coverage it reflects prejudices against persons of almost every social origin.

This is not the place to review the studies on prejudices in instructional materials. The literature on this subject is considerable and extends over a number of decades. Recent studies show that in children's fiction Negro boys and girls are still depicted as unambitious and accepting defeat.[6] Negroes are shown as slaves, cooks, and handymen, and seldom as business or professional men or executives. In other words, the "traditional" image of the Negro is still depicted in some of the literature from which children form their concepts and attitudes.

In recent years attempts have been made to develop multi-ethnic reading books for children in the common schools.[7] In these books an integration of ethnic groups is presented and a genuine effort is made to eliminate the traditional prejudices. But when the books are analyzed, it becomes evident that they have not entirely succeeded. For example, when the content is classified as to the degree that success, failure, and help are emphasized in the stories, it turns out that in some of the books less than one-third of the stories depict success. In books that treat the white man alone, two-thirds of the stories are success stories. Stories that emphasize help occur frequently in some multi-ethnic books, showing a subtle bias not found in the materials prepared for an all-white series.

Subject matter may be biased by what it does *not* say as well as by what it says. The neglect of almost all minority groups in history texts is well known. Few elementary or high school teachers have a chance to study the contributions of minorities to American culture. They learn little of the contributions of the Chinese-, Japanese-, and Mexican-, as well as Negro-Americans to the life of the nation. And the original American, dispossessed and relegated to reservations, is almost forgotten except at moments when history books tell of his conquest by the white man.

The content of instruction may also be stacked against the laborer and his unions or the farmer and his problems. It may over-emphasize military figures and play down the contributions of artists to society. It may shun problems of sex and marriage and at the same time extol the values of family life. And the sectional and nationalistic slanting of content has often been remarked upon. In fact, few school subjects have escaped the pressure of one group or another to modify their content. Teachers are accountable for the objectivity of the content they teach. And a program that does not prepare them to examine the biases of instructional materials and to select subject matter as fair as possible to all interests and groups is inadequate.

CHAPTER 11

PREPARATION IN THE GOVERNANCE
OF THE PROFESSION

Just as he needs adequate preparation in the knowledge, attitudes, and techniques of teaching, so does the teacher need to understand the principles, policies, and procedures of his organized profession. In some professions, it may not be necessary for a trainee to study the procedures and policies of his professional organization because they are so simple anyone can gain a command of them through daily experience. However, this is not true of the profession of teaching. The teacher and his profession touch the public at so many vital points that the prospective teacher needs to study with care the issues that confront his profession. But before he can work confidently on these problems, he must answer the question of how the profession is to be organized and governed.

The question of what the prospective teacher should be taught about his profession and its government can be answered by reference to issues such as the autonomy of the teacher, or by presenting an outline of professional policies and procedures. Or it can be answered by reference to publications that set forth the status of teaching as a profession. Perhaps elements of all these approaches can be found in the following pages. But the emphasis here is upon how the profession should be perceived and how it should be organized and governed. For unless the profession can put its own house in order, clarify its own sense of direction, and establish its own policies and procedures, it will be ineffective in working with the public and its own members. Furthermore, feelings of self-esteem and commitment to the profession will be enhanced as teachers come to feel that the profession controls itself and is imbued with a sense of mission.

---

* This chapter was prepared in substance by David D. Darland of the National Commission on Teacher Education and Professional Standards.

Much is written about the self-esteem and commitment of teachers. But until the teaching profession establishes its own self-government and sets its own patterns of performance and evaluation, there will be too little commitment. The process is under way, but there is much confusion. At the moment there exists a condition which is best described as professional anarchy. The individual teacher often receives little support from his professional associations in his attempt to uphold the precepts of a professional.

This chapter sets forth the status of teaching as a profession, and presents a position on how the profession should be organized and governed, a position doubtless in conflict with the views of some teachers and some elements of the public. But to set forth a few *substantive* propositions on the question seems more desirable than giving a number of issues prospective teachers should consider. This approach offers something to examine; it opens up the issues in ways that questions alone cannot do.

A Concept of the Profession

If teachers are to have control of their own affairs, it is essential that a distinction be drawn between the control of education and the governance of the teaching profession. This assumes that this governance be delegated to a variety of professional organizations, agencies, boards, and commissions with clearly defined responsibilities. Such an entity will establish necessary checks and balances to protect the public interest as well as generate and disseminate the power of the teaching profession. Those who are the best qualified in any given aspect of a profession should be involved in the policy- and decision-making processes in the public interests. Contrary to popular opinion, public and professional interests are usually not in conflict.

The people of the United States are involved in a great social revolution. Teachers have habitually reflected, not led, the forces of society. The setting in which teachers find themselves today demands more dynamic and intelligent leadership, especially in the professionalization of teachers. Their professional integrity is at stake.

If the teaching profession is to acquire and maintain the intellectual strength and the political power necessary in these times, a new concept of the professional must be created. This concept must include new structures and functions—in short, a professional entity.

The importance of the control and proper support of education is inextricably involved with teaching. But the subject here is the teaching profession and its governance, rather than the control of education.

The social revolution in America directly affects the teaching profession. There are two concurrent, related power struggles. One is over who is to control education and the other is how and by whom the teaching profession is to be maintained and governed.

The teaching profession today is highly vulnerable. Because of its lack of maturity as a professional entity, there is neither the backlog of precedent nor adequate professional protection for those who wish to be heard on issues vital to education and the teacher. Of course, teachers should not control education, but they should be in a position to be heard, and they should govern their own profession.

Education at the elementary and secondary levels was organized before there was any semblance of an education profession. It became customary for lay boards not only to control education but to govern the profession of teaching. There was almost no distinction drawn between them. It is only recently that teachers have moved decisively toward professionalization. Yet in many areas laymen are still, today, having to make decisions of a professional nature. Control of the profession by laymen is so entrenched that it is very difficult to understand the importance of differentiating between control of education and governing of the profession. Acceptance of this difference is essential if the teaching profession is to function in the best interests of society.

It is this process of differentiation that is now causing so much concern. Precisely because teachers are moving rapidly toward maturing as a professional force, toward creating their own instruments of governance, is concern being voiced by the traditionalists.

The attention of teachers is easily diverted to the support of a professional organization as an end in itself. Jurisdictional conflicts are thus created. The organization becomes the end, and the internecine conflict among organizations consumes the energy and displaces constructive programs needed for development of an effective profession.

A concrete example is the AFT-NEA feud. This is not to say that the conflict is not real. It is. But it is peripheral to the issue of teaching becoming a professional entity, capable of responsible self-government. Organizations which use their energies to produce such an entity must ultimately receive the backing of the majority of teachers and of the American people. If this is true, there is strong reason for classroom teachers to recognize that jurisdictional battles are a waste of energy and that great professional issues go begging as long as this goal displacement prevails. When enough classroom teachers discover that it is they who are being weakened and divided, not school boards, college professors, or administrators, there will be a more vigorous thrust toward making teaching a professional entity.

Meanwhile, it is urgent that attention be given to evolving a conceptual design for a professional entity. This idea requires careful delineation and must be viewed in the context of its assumptions. Some of these assumptions are:

1. Teaching is a highly complex endeavor involving ever greater techniques and never-ending knowledge of the highest order.
2. Teaching requires continuous education relevant to the needs of the practitioner.
3. Teaching assumes the necessity of the involvement of practitioners in establishing their own patterns of self-improvement and patterns of professional governance. (Intrinsic motivation is essential.)
4. Teaching assumes that the vital point is what takes place between teacher and child or youth. (It involves both the affective and cognitive domains.)
5. Teaching assumes the need to have a supportive staff of specialists for the teacher to draw upon at all times for assistance.
6. Teaching assumes the inextricable relationship between the conditions in which children attempt to learn and a teacher to teach, and success in these endeavors.

The above list could be expanded but these assumptions are enough to illustrate the imperative need for the practitioners of all areas, levels, and specialties in the teaching profession to recognize that none of these can be accomplished unless there are ways to support them with continuing action programs. For example, perennial education for teachers will hardly be relevant to their needs unless teachers are involved in determining the nature of such education. And that requires professional government.

Currently, the teaching profession is composed of a loose federation of groups and individuals which operate quite independently. It is not uncommon for two groups to have a common, stated goal but, because of the professional anarchy which prevails, one group often neutralizes the other.

Ideally, the teaching profession should build an entity which ensures for all practitioners certain well defined rights and opportunities for effective service. Such an entity is not a single organization. It is rather a profession: a planned integration of interrelated individuals and groups with no fixed physical dimensions, each group with specialized functions, all directed toward common purposes.

In the teaching profession there are dozens of interests and forces to be reconciled. The anatomy or structure of the profession has been defined to include the segments and the practitioners within each segment listed below.

1. Those who teach or carry out other professional activities in preschool programs and in elementary and secondary schools.
2. Those who teach or carry out other professional activities in colleges and universities.

3. Professional personnel in state departments of education and other governmental agencies such as the United States Office of Education.
4. Professional personnel in organizations directly related to teaching at any level.
5. Professional personnel in voluntary accrediting agencies involved with accreditation of educational institutions.[1]

Each of the groups mentioned functions in the setting of noncommercial institutions, professional agencies, or governmental agencies. The term "teacher" is used to include all members of the teaching profession and is differentiated from the term "classroom teacher."

The setting in which teachers are employed appears to have had rather profound influence on them. For example, a recent survey[2] reveals that persons employed in elementary and secondary settings tend first to be *loyal to their individual school (or system)*; second, to their level or area of teaching; and only third to the precepts and commitment of the profession. One might be a little uneasy if one felt that such a condition prevailed in medicine.

There is considerable evidence that provincialism is a strong force among teachers: for example—

1. the mutual distrust between people from lower education and higher education,
2. the state and regional loyalties that emerge at any national educational forum,
3. the fact that the teaching profession tends to pattern its organization upon the way in which *education is organized* rather than create a new pattern which is independent and autonomous.

The last point is especially troublesome. Great reliance is placed upon the role of local teacher organizations and their relationships with local boards of education in matters which far transcend the capability of much of the currently established professional machinery. Of course, local professional groups could handle many of their own professional problems if they had clear, well defined, and fixed responsibilities. For example, they could develop and carry on an agreed-upon perennial education program, designed by and for teachers.

There is a multiplicity of professional matters that cannot be satisfactorily handled at a local level: for example, serious cases involving competence and ethics. Here the profession must depend upon peer judgment, but such judgment should be made by those outside the setting of the problem and not personally acquainted with or professionally related to the institution involved. Teachers must have professional protection and responsibilities and commitments which transcend their local systems, but there is still a great need for strong local professional groups. These require machinery for professional governance managed by professionals and sanctioned by law. Such a plan does not deny the important role of local groups but illustrates the importance of a design of operation different from and independent of the way education is organized and controlled.

Today there are few considerations more important to a profession than a standard of living which allows a practitioner to have job security and to build an adequate retirement. Security once vested in property is now vested in job security and retirement, but so far the teaching profession has not adjusted to this change. In a country where teachers must be mobile, little attention is paid to the need for a universal retirement system which makes crossing state boundaries irrelevant. Few teachers even dream of independence in such matters. The best retirement plan for teachers to date sets up reciprocal relationships among states permitting teachers to transfer or buy into state retirement systems.

The teaching profession should design a true retirement system whereby employer and employee contributions are placed in individual accounts and held there until retirement or death. Some large business corporations do this without letting state boundaries inhibit them. But the teaching profession is so tied to the way education is organized that it behaves as though its own pattern must be consonant with that of the state system. After all, the thinking goes, education is a state function.

Teachers are equally inhibited by the fact that teaching is a "public" profession. Therefore, it follows that the "public" may decide upon professionally technical matters such as certification of teachers and evaluation of teachers. But these decisions should be made by the ones best qualified to make them in the interest of the public welfare. If teaching were already a professional entity, such decisions would be made without question by the professionals.

It is important to keep in mind that what is being advocated here is the idea that a profession should govern itself and assume the responsibility for decisions best made by professionals. Of course, the control of all professions is ultimately vested in the people. But the delegation of rights and responsibilities to a profession has substantial precedent in our society. To delegate such rights either by agreement, law, or precedent does not mean that the people give up these rights. It is, of course, implicit that when the right of professional governance is afforded any given profession, it be upon the premise of built-in guarantees, so that self-serving zeal does not supersede the public welfare. This is why the teaching profession must be a functioning entity rather than a monolithic organization. The very nature of successful teaching derives from the involvement which the process of self-government provides. This is the essence of intrinsic motivation which provides the dynamics of self-fulfillment, improvement, productive change, and intellectual liberation.

A Design for a Self-Governing Entity

Since structure and machinery should accommodate function, we will begin with the essential functions of any profession in our society and attempt to evolve a workable concept of professional entity.

Function 1. Educating for the profession. A profession depends to a large degree on a wide range of intellectual abilities to carry on its services. Furthermore, professional education and training must be continuous if competency is to be maintained. Educating teachers should be viewed as a never-ending function of the profession, and designs for accomplishing such a function should be created.

The details involved are not relevant here but the great number of vested interests are. These include the interests of educational personnel from each of the settings in which teachers serve, as discussed above.

Local school personnel, especially classroom teachers, are particularly concerned, since they are often expected to supervise teachers-in-training in addition to carrying a full teaching load. Very little effort has been directed toward organizing programs for the initial preparation of teachers so that mature practitioners working with teachers-in-training, or interns, are assigned such responsibility as a part of their regular teaching load. This function is typically assigned to a teacher *in addition* to his regular teaching responsibilities. This would not be the case if the teaching profession had charge of its own affairs. Currently, there is some interest in providing school systems which assist in teacher preparation with a differential state grant of money for classroom teachers to work with prospective teachers as a part of their regular teaching load. This will be done only if the profession presses the issue; it serves here to illustrate the type of issue in which the organized teaching profession must become more involved.

In the future, some initial preparation of teachers should be done in training cadres of people for a variety of educational positions. The Education Professions Development Act emphasizes the importance of preparing education personnel in teams. This implies the acceptance of the concept of differentiation of staff and of experimentation with the deployment of educational talent, both designed to provide greater opportunity for individual programs of study and learning for children and youth.

Such a concept requires a new emphasis on the interrelationships between professional personnel in teacher education institutions and in the schools. Not only are such relationships necessary for the initial preparation of teachers, but they are necessary to build relevant perennial education programs for teachers. A profession should surely be responsible for policies governing the adequate initial preparation of personnel and those governing further education for its members.

Function 2. Maintaining machinery for policy formulation and decision making for the educating of teachers. The people have delegated the primary control of education to state legislatures and state departments of education. Local boards have been delegated certain parallel and specific powers. But the right to educate, certify teachers, and accredit teacher training institutions rests with the state government. It is important to remember here that local school boards are also the creations of the state government.

In the interests of the public welfare and the teaching profession, the following teacher education functions in each state should be delegated to the teaching profession:

1. the licensure of teachers
2. the revocation or suspension of license procedures
3. the review of waiver of any certification requirements
4. the accreditation of teacher education institutions
5. the power to develop suggested programs, studies, and research designed to improve teacher education, including advanced education of teachers.

These functions, with few exceptions, are now vested in the respective state departments of education* which are most often controlled by lay boards. The legal right and power to establish policies, develop procedures, and make decisions regarding the functions mentioned above should be vested in a professional standards board in every state. A few states have moved in this direction, but there is great reluctance to ask that such responsibilities be placed in the hands of professionals.

For purposes of interrelation and coordination, the administrative officer of such boards should be an ex-officio member of the staff of the state department of education, and the staff should be housed in state department offices. There should be clear recognition, however, of the importance of the staff's responsibility to the teaching profession. Rather detailed guidelines for establishing such boards[3] are already in existence.

It should be clear that the major responsibility of any such board would be policy formulation and decision-making power over the administrative machinery that carries out the above functions. Since these boards would be creatures of state legislatures, they would be under constant legislative review. This is a very substantial check

---

* The state department of education, as used here, is a collective term including the chief state school officer, his professional staff, and the respective state boards of education (in states having such boards).

on any profession. But the technical dimensions of the functions under consideration require the attention of the professionals who are wholly responsible.

Obviously, teacher education, certification, and accreditation are three separate functions and should be administered as such. Each should continue to have its separate machinery. Teacher education should be vested with higher education institutions in cooperation with the common schools. Institutions should be afforded greater autonomy and should be encouraged to experiment with new programs of teacher education. Teacher certification and the accreditation of preparatory institutions should reflect this flexibility.

An important function of a professional standards board would be to encourage the creation of study and research teams preparing teachers for the various educational levels and academic areas of teaching. This would provide opportunity for meaningful involvement of liberal arts personnel.

As teaching becomes a more mature profession, quite probably there will be only an initial licensure. Advanced standings in level of teaching or specialties will be administered and controlled by the appropriate specialty group. Professional standards boards should have the power to experiment with such procedures. It would be interesting, for example, if every state in the union had a broadly representative study and research team working on the improvement of programs for training mathematics teachers. The same could be said for all parallel academic and specialty groups.

Everyone in teaching knows that accreditation of teacher education continues to be a complex problem. Recently the Mayor study[4] reaffirmed the need for the National Council for the Accreditation of Teacher Education (NCATE). Nevertheless, there is much foot-dragging in this matter. If the profession were really in charge of its own affairs in the various states, accreditation could probably become national, as in other professions.

Function 3. Establishing and maintaining machinery for protection of competent and ethical teachers, establishing tenure, and protecting the public welfare. Few things are more in the public interest than the protection of the continuity of service of competent and ethical teachers. This requires tenure laws as well as administrative machinery where the profession assumes responsibility for the protection and discipline of its own ranks.

There should be in each state an effective tenure law, administered by a legally established professional practices commission composed of personnel broadly representative of the profession. It is widely held that tenure laws overprotect the incompetent teacher. Many people charge, in tenure cases involving competence, that another person, often an administrator, is placed on trial rather than the accused. This may well be the case because there are few well established procedures for due process involving tenure cases. But the minimums for such due process are well known and well established in other areas of national life, although too often representative professional personnel are only indirectly involved.

Most tenure laws for teachers are obsolete; they need constant revision. But a backlog of useful precedent is developing, and there are some recent innovations which are proving helpful. One is a change in an Oregon law permitting a tenure teacher, who is charged, the right to a professional hearing before a body of his peers before any recommendation is made to the hiring agency. This procedure may be worth following elsewhere.

It is important that every teacher have the right of hearing before his peers. This can be accomplished by a legally established professional practices commission, in each state, with the power to subpoena witnesses and hold hearings as prescribed by law. This procedure can protect as well as discipline or eliminate the incompetent. An effective commission probably requires a frame of reference, such as a code of ethics, as a point of departure in ethics cases. A code which has been ratified by most educational groups whose members are likely to be involved already exists.

A frame of reference is also needed as an orientation in answering questions of competency. Such a framework would necessarily be broadly gauged because competency will vary with individual cases. There is not substantial precedent in this area, but a backlog of rulings will grow as commissions are established and begin to function effectively. Several states have made beginnings in this direction, but most of these do not connect tenure law with the responsibilities of such commissions.

Function 4. Establishing and maintaining the machinery for the profession to negotiate collectively with hiring agencies regarding matters of welfare, conditions of work, and all matters affecting the effectiveness of teachers. The right to collective bargaining or to professional negotiation is being universally demanded by teachers. The right of organizational jurisdiction for such collective action has become a most bitter battleground.

The great controversy in this matter has prompted some to consider adopting a plan now operating in eight provinces of Canada. In each province, all certified teachers must automatically belong to their respective provincial teachers' federation as well as to the Canadian Federation of Teachers. Provincial federations are authorized and directed to develop collective bargaining procedures and assist local units in bargaining. Provisions are made for impasses, but they seldom occur. It is interesting to note that in several provinces the same law requires the teachers' federation to lobby in the provincial legislature for better education.

With regard to the right to negotiate, few actions taken by teachers anywhere have incurred greater wrath. Teachers are being accused of turning their backs on the children. They are said to be militants without altruistic cause, interested only in their own welfare. But teachers have for years, through low salaries and the loss of adequate retirement, been subsidizing the education of their pupils. The economic plight of teachers is overt and obvious. Because of the close tie-in with the finance of education, property taxes, and local politics, teachers must necessarily be concerned with their own welfare.

However, there are many other aspects of teaching where collective action is needed and is proceeding. These include conditions of work, teacher assignment, perennial education, leave policies, clerical assistance, and the assistance of teacher aides.

Function 5. Maintaining effective professional organizations. Teachers' organizations in the United States are in a revolutionary transition. In both major national teacher groups—the NEA and the AFT and their affiliates—there is obvious turmoil. The one-man, one-vote Supreme Court decision will very likely change the nature of state legislative bodies. Urbanization will be more and more in evidence in these bodies. This will affect state educational organizations, their policies, and programs. Moreover, the breakthrough at the federal level, in more open-ended financial support, the civil rights laws, the 18-year-old vote movement, city renewal, the move for decentralization of city schools, and similar forces, will greatly condition the nature and programs of national education associations, learned societies, and other such organizations.

Moreover, as the evidence mounts that many public schools are not only inadequate but in many cases failing, especially in the inner city, teachers' organizations will realize that they must become more and more concerned with changing the system.

Teachers must become much more concerned with education in general, not merely formal and institutional education. The lack of adequate access to instruments of mass communication for educators is a major deterrent to more effective educational effort. Teachers have not felt enough professional security to battle effectively in the political arena. When issues are outside the halls of formal education, educational groups tend to follow a hands-off policy. Teachers' organizations have only recently been willing to be counted among vested interest groups, even though democracy depends and thrives on open and constant struggle among such groups.

Education associations are almost notorious in their defense of the *status quo* in education. Historically, they have spent much more time in this endeavor than in helping teaching to become a major profession. Moreover, teachers seldom distinguish between education per se and the distinctly different matter of governing their profession. Even constructive criticism of schools is likely to be viewed by teachers as an attack upon themselves. The overwhelming percentage of education association budgets is spent on matters directly related to education and very little on putting the profession's house in order. Both are important, but teachers have neglected their own professionalization.

Accordingly, associations should place a higher priority upon creating a well defined and functioning entity for the teaching profession. These associations cannot carry out all the functions necessary for a self-governing profession, but they can create the design and cause such governance to be established.

There are certain minimum functions for which a profession must assume responsibility. These functions must be viewed ecologically and must be defined and fixed accordingly.

Teachers might work for the development and passage of, in each state legislature, a single professional regulations act for teachers which will do the following:

1. Establish a single organization for certified* educational personnel in each state in which membership is mandatory. This organization will be responsible for developing appropriate subunits, and will have the specified legal responsibility to:
   a. work to improve local, state, and national education,
   b. work for the welfare of teachers at the local, state, and national levels,
   c. negotiate with local boards for salaries and all welfare matters,
   d. negotiate with local boards regarding policies and conditions which influence teaching effectiveness,
   e. establish a system of grievance procedures,
   f. establish an equitable local, state, national dues system,
   g. maintain an appropriate and adequate professional staff, and
   h. carry on research in the improvement of the professional entity of the teaching profession.
2. Establish a professional standards board, broadly representative of the profession, appointed by the governor. This board should be autonomous and independent of any association, organization, or institution. Its function would be to establish

* Membership should be open to noncertified personnel who are directly involved in any aspect of teacher education, governmental education work, or on accreditation staffs, or professional associations' staffs. (Includes all who teach at higher education levels.)

and administer procedures for each of those responsibilities mentioned on page 142 related to licensure and accrediting of teacher education.

3. Establish tenure regulations and an autonomous and independent professional practices commission, broadly representative of the profession and appointed by the chief state school officer. This commission should administer tenure law and protect and discipline members of the profession when necessary.

4. Establish and authorize a universal retirement system for teachers.

5. Establish Save-Harmless Laws (affording protection to teachers in negligence cases).

There are undoubtedly other practice regulations which would be added as times goes on. Items 1 through 5 above are an attempt to suggest a legal basis for the teaching profession as an entity.

It is suggested that state organizations be assigned responsibility for negotiating with local boards. This assumes the use of local negotiating teams. It is obvious that an appeal system of several levels is a necessity. There is a growing body of literature on this subject since several states have moved toward establishing local negotiating teams. The idea of negotiation assumes mutual trust, and decision making should be kept at the level of those directly involved. However, if an impasse occurs, there should be machinery provided to cope with it. But such machinery should encourage diligent negotiation at the initial level.

To date, no state has established the legal requirements of one single organization as indicated in item 1, but the idea is being discussed and, though very controversial, it is not without precedent.

It has been stated here that a professional entity is more than an organization. There should be no monolithic control over a profession. Accordingly, items 2 and 3 recommend *two separate, autonomous, independent bodies,* one appointed by the governor to deal with licensure and accreditation of teacher education, and the other appointed by the chief state school officer to deal with tenure, competence, and ethics. These would provide the necessary system of checks and balances.

Obviously, any professional regulations act will have to be carefully written so that various boards and commissions do not have conflicting legal jurisdictions. The number of such state bodies should be held to a minimum. This also argues for a single act covering all the practice regulations for teachers, including the financing and administration of such activities.

But if teaching has a legal undergirding this does not mean that there exists a professional entity. There is a multiplicity of functions which are voluntary, extralegal, and assigned by tradition: for example, the initial preparation of teachers, research activities, lobbying for better education, and curriculum improvement. In short, there are roles and responsibilities being accepted by several types of institutions, agencies, and organizations in the interests of the teaching profession. There is a need for all of these, but their roles and responsibilities must be rethought. The roles and responsibilities of teacher organizations are in great transition. No one doubts that all levels of organization are essential, but clarification of roles, interrelationships, and responsibilities is direly needed. If states were to systematize the legal undergirding of the teaching profession this would give new emphasis to organizational élan.

If something like the above were established in each state,* then the work at the national association level would assume new dimensions and would be more assertive in other areas. A profession has universal dimensions. Accordingly, some national accreditation of teacher education must become universal, but states must be involved. If each state did have a professional standards board, such a board might endorse accreditation of teacher preparation institutions by NCATE. NCATE is already approved by the majority of state departments of education in the United States. It should be remembered that NCATE is governed by an independent and broadly representative professional group. Accordingly, under such adjusted auspices for accreditation of teacher education in states, the national association's work would take on renewed importance in encouraging more productive procedures, studies, and experimentation.

A national association should meet the exigencies of unexpected problems related to the profession. This requires much greater agility than has been the case. Such an association would continuously run seminars directed to anticipate problems. In addition, financial reserves should be held to facilitate the convening of *ad hoc* professional specialists to meet exigencies. No professional staff can accommodate all such needs. But, when problems arise which are outside its competence, the staff should know the best and wisest persons to consult. Such organizational agility will require some serious rethinking on the part of most members of the teaching profession.

At the moment there is considerable emphasis upon a variety of forms of decentralization of inner-city schools. The implication of this for teachers is considerable. To cope with related professional problems will require strong local, state, and national approaches.

---

*Several states have some of the above already established, but no state requires a single organization and mandatory membership. Some confusion exists as to interrelationships of existing bodies.

Each level will have a role to play. But teachers need not fear such educational reforms if they are organized to protect the precepts of the profession.

It is the individual practitioner who needs desperately to be heard on the variety of professional matters which affect him. He cannot hope to be heard without established channels and procedures. A major function of organization should be to bring into being a professional entity. This process has begun, but it is being done piecemeal and often without a view of the whole. Teaching will never be as effective as it should be until it governs itself.

CHAPTER 12

TEACHER EDUCATION AS PERENNIAL

Preparation of the teacher can begin as far down the scale of professional competence as the teacher aide, but there is no upper limit to the preparation he can have. As long as knowledge about education continues to increase and new techniques and devices are contrived, there will be something new for the teacher to learn regardless of his degree or years of experience. The continuum of preparation can therefore cover the teacher's entire career.

That part of the continuum that precedes certification is ordinarily referred to as preservice training. Preparation beyond this is called "in-service training," or more recently, "continuing education." We shall use the term "perennial education." This expression will be used because not all of a teacher's education after certification is acquired in service, and because the expression "continuing education" has been preempted by those who are concerned with schooling below the bachelors degree level. The line separating the two phases of a teacher's education is tenuous and useful primarily in fixing responsibilities for formulating and carrying on programs of training.

The Purpose of Perennial Teacher Education

The purpose of the perennial education of teachers is to increase the proficiency of teachers now employed. The roles of teachers, their prior preparation, and their career aspirations vary so greatly that a program of perennial education must serve a number of specific needs and goals. Among other goals, the program should:

—remedy the teacher's deficiencies arising out of defects in his initial teacher-training preparation),

—advance the teacher's skills and pedagogical knowledge required for new teaching roles,

—advance and update the teacher's knowledge of subject matter, and

—train the teacher for non-tutorial positions.

A brief exploration of each of these will help to clarify and justify these goals.

Present programs of teacher education emphasize conceptual information separate from its use, and give little attention to training in the techniques and skills required in the teacher's work. As a result, the teacher's further education must often be remedial. Instead of preparing the teacher to perform at an advanced level of proficiency, perennial education must, therefore, often discipline him in the basic elements of teaching he missed. This deficiency is crucial among teachers in deprived areas who often lack understanding and appreciation of the interests, attitudes, mannerisms, and backgrounds of the children. In fact, most of their education has probably given them a picture of the schools that is in sharp contrast to the realities of the ghettos and rural poverty. Furthermore, training in the skills necessary to work with disadvantaged pupils and their parents, or, for that matter, any group of pupils or parents, has been practically omitted in the teacher's program of preparation. For these reasons, programs of perennial education should focus on the correction of faulty habits of interacting with children and parents. The programs should begin with a diagnosis of the teacher's behavior and move to the activities and training situations that will bring about an improvement in his performance.

If the level of teaching proficiency indicates that remedial work is unnecessary, the teacher's further education can then focus upon more advanced preparation. The demand for teachers is so great that it is not possible to train the teacher at the initial level in all the skills and understandings he will need in his career. Only through programs of perennial education can he acquire the more complicated skills and explanatory concepts and principles he will need as he advances into differentiated teaching roles, such as master teacher, teacher trainer, and supervisor of interns. A program of perennial education for this purpose should be stocked with an ample supply of advanced training situations and with protocol materials that require a deeper and more penetrating analysis than those used at the initial level of preparation.

What has just been said about the advanced training of the teacher can be said about the teacher's knowledge of subject matter. The preservice preparation of the teacher in the subject matter of instruction must necessarily be less than is needed for effective teaching. While he will continue to learn more and more about the content as he teaches it, a program of perennial education should make accessible to the teacher additional knowledge that he will need in his career. Furthermore, multiplication of knowledge goes on at a rapid pace. Even though the greater proportion of information from research becomes insignificant after a brief period, the amount of lasting knowledge from research and scholarship is nevertheless large; some of this can be of use to teachers. The further education of the teacher should, therefore, serve two purposes in the area of his subject matter preparation. It should deepen and broaden his knowledge and update his information.

During their careers, many teachers find themselves becoming interested in aspects of school work for which they have little or no specific training. For example, a teacher may be encouraged by the administration to become a counselor or a supervisor or he may decide on his own to become a school psychologist or a social worker. Such new interests will lead him into new responsibilities. Programs of perennial education should make ample provision to obtain the appropriate preparation.

Critique of Existing Programs

Programs of perennial education in the universities and colleges are often chaotic. In summer schools and extramural programs, the teacher typically takes courses to satisfy the university or college requirements for a master's degree. Except for one or two required courses (in some schools, none), the teacher may take from the course offerings whatever is convenient or appeals to his fancy. He may take a course in administration, one in guidance, one in educational psychology, another in secondary education, and sometimes a course or two in a subject matter discipline. The work he takes usually does not prepare him to be better at the tasks that arise on his job, or, for that matter, to perform any tasks at all.

In far too many institutions, the preparation beyond his preservice training is not directed to the improvement of his performance. This absence of direction occurs partly because perennial education is geared to increases in salary which are not related to proficiency but to the number of credit hours or equivalent experience that a teacher has accumulated. A bachelor's degree is worth so much on the schedule; a bachelor's degree plus a master's is worth an additional amount; and a master's plus additional credit hours calls for still further increases in salary. The assumption is that all courses of equal credit are of equal value—to some extent, a valid assumption. Since some courses are unrelated to improvement of the teacher's skills and techniques or to his ability to interpret situations or to take part in educational controversies, they are equally valuable because they are equally worthless as professional preparation.

This tendency of experienced teachers to sample courses is reinforced by the doctrine that each teacher is so unique in capacity, prior learning, experience, and interests that his program should be tailor-made by him and his advisor. The data needed to do this are, alas, lacking. But more important is the fact that the first purpose of teacher education is to protect the clients of the school against incompetence, not to develop the teacher as a person. That is the primary task of general education. Naturally, choices among courses should be allowed when they are in line with the teacher's career goals, but these must always be made within a program designed to discipline the teacher in the knowledge and techniques essential to his competence. To allow the programs of individual teachers to be determined entirely by their advisors without benefit of a general program of specified requirements is irresponsible. In an institution where the faculty is so confused about teacher education that no collective judgment is possible, where the faculty has taken the idea of individual differences so seriously that it thinks this applies with equal force to general and professional education, such irresponsibility could occur.

The lack of connection between perennial education and improvement in performance can be attributed also to the failure of higher institutions to devise programs of advanced training. They provide courses in pedagogy and in the disciplines, but these are too often designed with little reference to the various roles that teachers play. Furthermore, these courses are not grouped and ordered so as to lead progressively to more effective performance in specified roles and positions.

The institutes established for teachers of the disadvantaged under the National Defense Education Act attempt to break away from formal courses and to gear the work to the instructional needs of experienced elementary and secondary teachers. So far as these institutes have taught the subject matter relevant to the needs of disadvantaged children (and few of them have done so), they have provided functional preparation for experienced teachers. They have been helpful in preparing the teacher to understand the children of deprived communities and the conditions under which they live. But they have been woefully lacking in any plan for systematically training the teacher in the skills and techniques that will enable him to be successful with children regardless of their backgrounds.

In a study of NDEA Institutes for teachers of the disadvantaged made by the Bank Street College of Education there were twice as many comments made about the understanding acquired as there were about the techniques the participants learned.[1] This is about the ratio one would expect since the orientation of Institute staffs is in the direction of reading and discussing issues rather than practice in the techniques of teaching. There is little support in the Institute faculties for serious consideration of training the teacher in the skills and techniques that he must master to be successful. In fact, the

Bank Street College study points out that the directors of Institutes believe that teachers will find a way to deal with their instructional problems if they have the desire and an appreciation of the child's situation.

This trust in inspiration and devotion partly explains the failure of most programs to bring about school improvements. It does little good for a teacher to understand that he should accept the child and build on what he is if the teacher does not know how to assess what the child brings and lacks the skills necessary to work with him. Acceptance and respect for a child as a human being, belief in his potential, and understanding of his social and emotional situation are all very good when they are expressed in appropriate teaching performances. In the abstract they are little more than pious expressions. The experienced teacher in search of help in his efforts to work more effectively with children might in justice lament, "Show me not the end without the means."

The National Teacher Corps has been in effect for so short a time that assessments of it are somewhat premature. From descriptions of its programs, the Corps is likely to founder on the same rocks as other programs. Its programs contain many conventional features: courses in psychology and sociology of education, and field experiences, clinical experience, and sensitivity training. The corpsmen work in small groups with a master teacher. While much of the corpsman's work is carried on in the community, his training is usually centered at a college or university. As in the Institute programs, much can be said for these features. But again there is the conspicuous absence of persistent training in the procedures and techniques of teaching and of interaction with pupils and parents. There is opportunity for observation and interaction with children and adults. But the programs do not provide adequately for training in the analysis of observations and for correction of practice in the light of feedback. The same defects found in student teaching are repeated here in an even more complex and demanding situation.

Teacher education suffers from blind confidence in the values to be derived from pooling personal experiences in group discussions. This procedure is worth least when teachers meet in local workshops led by supervisors, principals, or teachers themselves. It is questionable enough when information is piped in from the outside by consulting personnel. There is no creative process, and certainly no group mind, that can raise the level of thought above that which is fed into a discussion. The more difficult the problems a group faces and the less competent its members, the more worthless is the process of pooling personal experience.

There is no doubt that group discussions of this order have some therapeutic effects. Individuals may feel better for having participated in a group and having said what they wished others to hear. It may also be true that teachers pick up different ideas and occasionally learn about some new technique or procedure. But no amount of mental massaging is a substitute for a program of systematically worked out instruction and practice in the interpretation of behavior and in the skills and techniques for working with children and adults of the community.

Toward Better Programs of Perennial Education

Perennial education cannot be focused upon one goal. It must provide for those who wish to increase their proficiency, for those who wish to prepare themselves for some new role in the school system, and for those who are trying to equip themselves to deal more effectively with day-to-day problems. Perennial education programs must be differentiated and the distinctions as to their nature and goals should be made clear. Just as there is a specific program for one who wishes to become a counselor or a speech correctionist, so there should be a definite program for individuals who want advanced training as elementary teachers, secondary teachers, master teachers, or supervisors of interns. This is the logical alternative to the helter-skelter preparation that most teachers are now receiving as they pursue work beyond the bachelor's degree.

Specialized programs will of course be centered in institutions of higher learning. But since a considerable proportion of the program will be carried on in the training complexes, the cooperation of the public schools will be needed in addition to the training facilities of the complex.

In addition, the teacher should have knowledge and skills that equip him to work with other teachers and members of the community. He is more than a classroom teacher. He is caught in a welter of issues today about the purposes of the school and the relation of the school to society. He may even become involved in controversies about the desirability of the educational system itself. He is almost certain to be called on to defend his professional practices. In order to handle these issues with insight and persuasion in a professional manner, the teacher must be disciplined in the elements of educational philosophy, psychology, and sociology that bear upon the school's relationship to the welfare of the people. Furthermore, the teacher must be prepared to meet demands for improvements in the educational system—to plan for change, to devise and follow effective strategies, to prepare the environment for intervention.

Traditionally, the teacher has been shielded from the harsh realities of public controversy about education. When these realities were faced by the profession, it was the administrator and educator who bore the brunt of the attack and the burden of defense. But the unionization of teachers and the involvement of the unions in an expanding range of educational issues make it necessary for the teacher to be not only professionally competent but also versed in the basic issues of our time and capable of influencing educational opinion in his community.

A teacher who is prepared to participate in his professional duties at this level will have had extensive work in systematic courses in educational psychology, educational philosophy, educational sociology and anthropology, and in the economics and politics of the educational system. By becoming steeped in educational ideas and by analyzing educational issues and matters of public policy in depth, the teacher acquires some of the competence that educational leadership in these times demands of him.[2]

Further Preparation for Teachers of the Disadvantaged

Because of the failure of teacher education programs to prepare teachers to work effectively with children regardless of their social origins, it is necessary to discuss the further training of teachers who will work, or are now working, in deprived areas or who will be teaching for the first time in integrated schools. This sort of further training will not be needed, of course, when teacher education is reformed along the lines suggested in the preceding chapters. What is suggested here are simply stopgap measures.

In deprived areas, additional training is needed for two groups of teachers: those who will be teaching in these areas for the first time, and those who are now teaching there and need further preparation to do their work more effectively. In the first of these two groups will be some who have not taught before as well as experienced people who have been teaching in suburbia or in other schools outside the rural slums and the ghettos. For the beginning teacher, the training should be designed with two purposes in mind. First, it should introduce teachers to the deprived communities and to the schools and, second, it should increase their skill in classroom work and in their interactions with parents, faculty, and other members of the community. If these two purposes are fulfilled, the probability that those so trained will continue to teach in these schools will be increased. But since other factors weigh heavily in determining how long an individual will teach in a school, the teacher's pertinacity may be only slightly affected.

The initial preparation should be given during the summer and cover approximately two months. Until training complexes are established, the next best modes of preparation would be intensive workshops or institutes.

The instruction should be as realistic as possible. This can be done by the situational approach to the teaching of theory, supplemented by visits to the schools and community. The protocol materials should contain the kinds of situations that the teachers will actually confront in the schools. The purpose of studying these materials is to develop the teacher's understanding of the behavior of children and to reduce the possible shock of becoming a part of social situations to which he is not accustomed. Because preparation must be given in a relatively short time, the protocol materials should be restricted to problems that most commonly baffle teachers in deprived communities. The protocol materials should therefore be weighted with situations in which there arise problems of classroom control plus those which help the teacher understand the attitudes, language, and modes of thought of the children. In this initial period some attention should be given to situations involving problems of instruction. But the time devoted to this aspect of the teacher's work would be comparatively small.

These beginning teachers should be given an intern status and assigned no more than a half-time teaching schedule, at least during the first year. They should be under the supervision of a training staff and continue to meet at scheduled times, either in the training complex or a workshop specially provided for them. The program should deal with problems encountered in their work. Samples of their classroom performance should be recorded as a basis for diagnosing their difficulties. The instruction and training situations should be designed to provide the understanding and skills in which they are deficient.[3]

The experienced teacher who will be working in a deprived area for the first time should be given the same sort of preparation the beginning teacher receives during the summer. His training should continue through the year and be like that of the beginning teacher, but it need not be as extensive.

The idea that the teacher in the schools of deprived communities understand the children and their social environment is erroneous. These teachers need to develop not only further skills and techniques for working with children and their parents but also the knowledge to comprehend the social circumstances of the children, their habits and attitudes. Again, the further education of the experienced teacher should be carried on through the use of protocol materials and training situations. The present practice of merely *talking* about the community and its problems and the children and their problems, and reading and studying about these matters from books, supplemented by visitations and a few films, is inadequate. Nor will the teacher of the disadvantaged pupil gain a great deal from formal courses on the psychological and social aspects of life in the inner city unless the courses are preceded by a study of concrete situations, as depicted, for example, on audio and video recordings. In other words, it must not be assumed that, since he has had experience in the schools with deprived children, the teacher in the disadvantaged areas can gain from abstract courses all that he needs to improve his performance.

Discussions, formal courses, and reading do lead to new understanding and insight, but they develop no techniques of analyzing actual situations into their constituent elements, nor skill in the performances that are essential to handling situations. They are no substitute for persistent training with ample feedback and direction from an instructor. On the basis of what is known about training in general and about research on training in the field of education, there is little justification for institutes or other educative mechanisms that do not provide a training program.

Preparing the Teacher for Desegregation

Integration poses special challenges to the teacher, for it creates conditions in which his prejudices, be he black or white, are brought to the surface in ways often detrimental to the child and perhaps extremely disturbing to the teacher. Problems of classroom management, of making children feel wanted, and of instruction itself come up in a new context and with greater complexity in an integrated school. Unless teachers are adequately prepared to deal with these problems, integration is apt to overwhelm the faculty and administration with difficulties they had not anticipated, and for which they are ill prepared.

Too much emphasis on the problems that will arise with desegregation may cause the faculty to overreact to the new situation. But this possibility can be obviated by emphasizing that children are more apt to feel liked and important in a classroom that focuses on interesting work, that makes clear what, when, and how things are to be done, and that engages all pupils in work. In other words, the emphasis should be upon school as usual, with no fanfare about the fact of integration.

But even if desegregation is handled smoothly and without display, there will still be problems arising from the prejudices of teachers. It is not the purpose here to list all the difficulties that may crop up as a school system is desegregated, but a few are set forth as evidence of the need to give attention to the problems that arise in the transition to integration. Among them—

1. how to be fair in an integrated class. A teacher may unwittingly be unfair by ignoring a child, by being either overlenient or oversevere, or by evidencing low expectations. Or the teacher may be unfair by rating a child against the total group rather than noting the strides he has made when he is measured against where he was.

2. how to establish and maintain an atmosphere in which each child feels liked and respected. Children are quick to pick up cues that indicate whether a teacher likes them and respects them. For example, a child may notice that the teacher passes quickly over his effort at responding to a question, or shrugs his shoulders in response to what the child says. A child may note that the teacher pays more attention to a white child than he does to a black child, or more attention to a black child than to a white one. The words a teacher uses may be taken as cues to the teacher's attitude. If he fails to use the name of a child or refers to him as "Boy," or makes reference to black, however innocently, as being ugly, this may be taken by a black child as derogatory.

3. how to handle social events. The prejudices and biases of a teacher will certainly be exposed in a situation which involves the social mingling of the different groups of students at school parties, dances, and other social functions. In these situations, the biases and animosities of the community itself may become involved. The teachers should be prepared to handle such possibilities in a way not detrimental to the continued desegregation of the educational system. Some of the knottiest problems that a teacher and the school administration face will arise in this context. Explosive questions, like intermarriage and choice of associates, will most certainly be in evidence.

4. how to establish and maintain communication between white children and minority groups such as Mexicans, Indians, and Negroes. This may be an especially difficult problem to handle where the cleavage between white and black pupils has become pronounced because of the influence of outside groups upon the pupils. There are some situations in which black pupils will not permit another black pupil to have friends among the whites. If he persists in doing so, he will find himself in difficulties with his black friends and associates. The same happens to white children who attempt to establish friendships with black children.

5. how to handle routine classroom matters such as seating arrangements and distribution of materials. To separate pupils by social origins will arouse suspicions of racial prejudice. This would be the case even though an alphabetical arrangement should, by chance, lead to such a grouping. A teacher who persistently, for whatever reason, calls upon white children only, or black children only, to give out materials may in all probability be prejudiced in the eyes of his pupils.

6. how to handle disruptive behavior. Problems of classroom discipline are at best annoying to the teacher. But they become

more complex with the integration of the school. The teacher is then confronted with the question of whether his treatment of the white pupil, if the teacher is black, is fair; or, if the teacher is white, whether his treatment of the black pupil is beyond reproach. In some situations, the white teacher is hesitant to discipline the black pupil for fear of criticism by the child himself or of being faced by irate parents. The same condition holds for a black teacher who must discipline a white child. These are matters that may cut deeply into the relationships among teachers, pupils, and parents. They should be frankly faced by all three of the groups. A teacher needs to know how to respond to a black child who says, "You punish me because you are prejudiced." The black teacher also may find himself in a similar situation and be at a loss to know how to respond. He, too, needs help.

Bringing the Teacher Trainer Up to Date

Part of the difficulty of designing and operating a program for the perennial education of teachers is that those who are responsible are not adequately prepared for the job. They are well disciplined in the subject matter of their fields and are competent to deal with it in conventional ways. But this sort of knowledge and competence is no longer adequate. The teacher educator is well versed in the theories and techniques of curriculum development and instruction, but he is typically unprepared to conduct a program of training or to guide the experienced teacher in the techniques of analyzing the situations with which he deals in the classroom, school, and community.

Those who are responsible for the perennial education of teachers should also be provided with an in-service program.[4] They need to be "updated" in the knowledge and techniques of teacher training itself. This point is crucial in the training of teachers because no program can be more effective than the trainers themselves. The teachers in the common school who supervise and instruct teachers, the supervisors and directors of instruction who now engage in in-service education, and college instructors all need in-service education. The Triple-T Project of the United States Office of Education recognizes this problem and has, in a limited way, attempted to solve it.* But the scope of the problem is so great that anything short of a massive attack will do little more than provide a variety of approaches.

The preparation of the teacher of teachers is centered in the graduate schools of the universities and colleges. Consequently, the

---

* The Triple-T Project is an attempt to involve colleges and universities in a nationwide effort to develop programs to prepare college professors, public school supervisors, and administrators in the procedures and techniques of teacher training. The project was begun in 1968 but is hampered by lack of funds.

graduate frame of mind has shaped the programs for the preparation of teacher trainers. The tenacity with which the graduate mentality holds on to the program is clearly seen in the title given to the few departments and schools of education that have acquired a measure of autonomy. They chose to call themselves graduate schools of education. And even the professionalization of the program leading to the Doctor of Education degree was never quite pulled off. This so-called professional degree turns out to be a research degree with the same trappings as a Doctorate of Philosophy—preliminary examinations, theses, and other appropriate rituals. And, of course, non-pedagogical departments, being even more insensitive to teacher education, made little or no effort to gear their programs to the preparation of teacher training personnel. So any effort to reconstruct the programs of teacher trainers runs up against the plain fact that graduate faculties have shown little, if any, interest in the use of their disciplines for this purpose.

It should be emphasized that this lack of interest is not confined to the non-pedagogical faculties, for perhaps there is no group more oblivious to the problem of using its knowledge to train the teacher of teachers than the faculties of education. Like the faculties of universities in the British Commonwealth, faculties of pedagogy have been, and continue to be, preoccupied with the preparation of research workers. Almost every individual who is awarded either a Doctor of Education or a Doctor of Philosophy degree is prepared in the techniques of investigating his field and is led to think that this activity is the most important one for him to pursue. The fact that comparatively few individuals so schooled do engage in productive research seems to be no bar. These individuals, while they are trained to do research and to prepare papers for publication, typically find themselves employed in institutions where they are responsible for training teachers already in service as well as in preservice. While thus engaged, they try to carry on research or write articles and books that will help them to escape from this assignment as early as possible and climb to the level of the graduate faculty—where they themselves can engage in the process of preparing individuals to do research—who will in turn be employed to train teachers.

This is the state of affairs in the field of education and it is to be found in almost every discipline offered in the universities. The purpose here is not to deprecate in the least the importance of research. It is through research that knowledge increases and the performance of social functions is ultimately improved. No one can deny that it is through research that the practice of medicine, agriculture, engineering, and education have all been significantly improved in this century. But it is important to remember that knowledge can be used for more than the production of further knowledge. The mobilization of our educational resources to prepare personnel to train the teacher of teachers is now as great a national imperative as the training of research workers.

CHAPTER 13

MEMO ON MONEY AND ACTION

In so vast and complicated a task as the training of the nation's teachers, it is unlikely that anyone can suggest a plan of action that will meet with general approval. Even if the substance of the plan were accepted (which is most unlikely), the timing and order of its execution would most certainly run into opposition from one quarter or another. Yet the need for a comprehensive plan is so urgent and so crucial to the nation's future that one is moved to throw caution to the wind and outline a plan. With no further ado, we set forth the following plan of action.

Outlines of a Plan

The spheres in which planning at the national, state, and local levels should be undertaken are: (1) preparation of materials of instruction for teacher education, (2) training of university and public school personnel in using these materials, and (3) development of the institutional mechanisms through which the nation's teaching force can be trained.*

We have emphasized repeatedly the need for materials of instruction. This is the first and perhaps most fundamental sphere of action. Efforts to develop the second and third spheres would likely be abortive without the first. The history of program development in the public schools, as well as in teacher education, shows that any attempt to carry on a program of instruction in the absence of adequate materials is almost certain to fail. All too often those who had worked out new plans for teacher education attempted to put them into operation without the materials needed for their proper development. The teacher trainer was thus forced to improvise materials and

---

* The proposed AACTE National Center for Teacher Education could serve as the planning and coordinating arm of the teacher education community.

learning activities on the spot. The popularity of these innovations, when they have been accorded it, was due to their being carried on by successful men, not because the programs were successful. Attempts to transfer these new programs to other institutions usually failed because no one could be sure of what was done or how it was done. To safeguard against abortive efforts, materials of instruction must be produced which will:

—teach concepts used to interpret behavior
—teach concepts to enable the teacher-trainee to interpret the social context of the school and the community
—train prospective teachers in skills prerequisite to work as interns
—develop appropriate attitudes toward the teacher's self and others
—teach concepts of the teaching profession and concepts of the teacher's role in it
—teach concepts used to analyze, evaluate, and control the content of instruction.

The task of producing these materials is so vast in scope and so intricate in detail that no university alone, indeed, no university in cooperation with a school system, could likely perform it. In the first place, personnel in the schools and universities are already overburdened with the job of carrying on the existing program of instruction. To take on the additional responsibility would result in either the neglect of instruction or the production of poor materials. In the second place, production would have to be carried on as an overload. This would entail additional funds which universities and schools cannot supply in sufficient amount. Finally, the available talent in any university and school system combined is too limited for the task. The development of materials will require the services of top-flight persons in educational psychology, educational philosophy, educational sociology, guidance and counseling, secondary and elementary education, pedagogical procedures, and, in addition, specialists in content areas and in reading, art, music, and educational technology.

Perhaps the most promising way of meeting the above difficulties would be to approach the task regionally. Each university or college and the school systems of the region would be able to free a portion of the manpower needed to form an adequate number of production teams.

These teams would be employed most efficiently if they were deployed by types of tasks. One team might develop interpretive materials, another, skill-training materials, and still another, attitude materials. Other teams would prepare materials on subject matter analysis and other specialzed areas. Each team would require specialists in educational technology to advise it on the media most appropriate to the presentation of its materials.

The amount of time required to develop materials can hardly be estimated here with accuracy. But it seems reasonable to suppose that at least two years of intensive work by the various teams would be required to develop a minimum supply. Each team would have to start from scratch, for there is very little existing material to draw upon. Furthermore, samples of the materials should be tried out and revised, to safeguard the teams against the development of irrelevant and ineffective instructional situations.

To test materials is to use them in the training of prospective teachers. This would indicate that at least one training complex ought to be established in each region of the country as the production team's center of operation. The location of these complexes could be determined by reference to factors such as the mixture of social and ethnic backgrounds of the population and the cooperation of the community. While the teams of each complex could be allowed maximum freedom as they work out materials, they should work within a common frame of purposes and tasks. Within such a general framework there is room for all the creative ability that can be assembled.

As experience is gained in the process of setting up and operating these initial complexes, and as materials and personnel become available, additional complexes can be established in each region. While the personnel of each new complex will doubtless modify the materials and develop new instructional situations as experience indicates, their primary function would be to train teachers with the materials already prepared.

If we have learned anything about curriculum development, it is that materials alone are not sufficient for the operation of an instructional program. The personnel must be able to use the materials in the process of teaching. Only a very small number of persons in teacher education are adequately prepared to train teachers. Advanced graduate work in education has emphasized training to do research rather than to train teachers. And even those programs that have given attention to teacher training have prepared individuals to fit into the pattern of courses in methods and student teaching. As a result, there is a scarcity of persons who would be able to use the new teacher training materials effectively. To relieve this shortage of trained manpower, it would be desirable to form training teams from those who produced the materials plus other qualified individuals. These teams could be used to staff summer institutes to prepare training personnel from both higher institutions and public schools, and to help with the initiation and development of training complexes.

Trained manpower is as crucial a factor as materials of instruction in the development and operation of training complexes. Any drive to establish complexes faster than manpower can be prepared should be strongly resisted. This is one of the lessons learned from the establishment of regional curriculum laboratories and research and development centers. These new social devices, which have not always been well staffed, drain off manpower from the universities and colleges and divest them of part of their most able staff, in many cases without increasing their productivity. This pitfall should be avoided in public schools and universities as production teams are formed and complexes established.

How Much Will It Cost?

What will it cost to produce an adequate supply of teachers? This question may be reduced to a number of components: What will it cost to produce a minimum stock of instructional materials? To train the personnel to use them? To establish and maintain an adequate number of training complexes? These questions cannot be given hard and fast answers because data are not readily available. But some perspective may be gained by considering how much the present production of teachers is costing. Again, the answer will be somewhat indefinite and restricted to circuitous inferences because very few data on the cost of teacher education are available. Even within a particular institution, information on the comparative costs of educating elementary and high school teachers is not accessible; and comparison of the cost of producing a physics teacher with that of a history teacher, for example, has seldom been made. The figures given in the following paragraphs are at best approximations. But this admission does not vitiate our conclusions if we bear in mind that we are interested in the general financial picture rather than preciseness of the data.

Beginning teachers are now being produced at the rate of approximately 175,000 per year. How much does that cost? Perhaps the best answer can be given by reference to the American Association of University Professors salary rating scale for institutions of higher learning. Over a third of the annual crop of teachers is produced by institutions that fall at the D level of the scale or below. Almost seventy percent are prepared by institutions at or below the C level. This means that a little less than three-quarters of the nation's teachers are turned out by small liberal arts colleges, denominational schools, state teachers colleges, Negro colleges, and the small state colleges and universities for which financial support is comparatively low. Some of these institutions provide good teacher education programs by present standards. They often give considerable attention to the adjustment of instruction to individual deficiencies and provide teaching experiences comparable to those in the more highly rated institutions. However, the financial resources of these institutions are so meager that they cannot alter their programs without massive assistance from outside sources.

Most of these institutions, especially those at the D level or below, can spend no more than $800 per student per year, and some spend less. Few, if any, of the institutions at the C level can spend as much as $2,000 per student. This means that almost three-fourths of the nation's teachers are being trained at institutions whose expenditures per student per year range between $800 and $2,000, with the majority falling toward the bottom of the range. Since schools on the A and B levels of the AAUP scale are not noted for their support of teacher education as compared to support in other areas such as physics and chemistry, it is reasonable to assume that an average expenditure per student is allocated to teacher education of perhaps about $2,000 per student per year.

If we assume that the average expenditure per student in teacher education is about $1,000 per year for schools at the C level and below, the total cost per teacher in these schools at the end of four years is $4,000. In schools at the B level and above, the total cost per teacher is about $8,000, assuming an expenditure of about $2,000 per year per student. In other words, about seventy percent of the nation's annual production of teachers is turned out at a cost of approximately $4,000 per teacher or a total expenditure of $490,-000,000. The remaining thirty percent costs $420,000,000. Combining these two sums we get $910,000,000 as the estimated cost of producing each crop of 175,000 beginning teachers.

The average total cost per teacher is about $5,200. While the task of producing a teacher is not exactly comparable to the production of a medical doctor (a better comparison would be that between a doctor of education and a doctor of medicine), the comparative costs are interesting. It has been estimated that it costs $32,000 to turn out a beginning physician, or about six times the cost of a beginning teacher. Perhaps the quality of teacher education is as good as what the nation is paying for.

So much for the present picture. What of the proposed program? How much will it cost? Quality education will require the production of about 384,000 teachers annually. If we take what the A and B schools are spending per student per year as the base cost, the total expenditure would be $3,072,000,000 per annual output, or an increase of a little more than two billion dollars over what is now spent to produce 175,000 teachers. But this increase would fall short of the amount required to provide an adequate system of teacher education for the nation.

In an earlier chapter we estimated that 2,500 training complexes would be needed to train 384,000 teachers per year. We assume that each complex will enroll about 150 trainees and that one staff member for every five students is a proper ratio for thorough training. Each complex should therefore have an instructional staff of approximately thirty persons to train beginning teachers. Additional personnel would be needed to work with teacher aides and to provide for certain training aspects of a program of perennial education. If the average salary is estimated at $18,000 per year, the instructional personnel for beginning teachers alone would cost about $540,000 per year. Additional funds for staffing the programs for teacher aides and experienced teachers would be required. The cost of administration, laboratory materials and apparatus, building maintenance, and so on, must be added. It seems reasonable to estimate that the annual operating cost for each complex would be about $800,000, or a total of $2,000,000,000 for all the complexes combined. The average cost per beginning teacher per year in the training complex would be roughly $5,000, including prorated costs of administration and overhead.

If each trainee spends a full calendar year in the training complex and a minimum of three years' study at a college or university, the total cost per teacher would be about $11,000, assuming $2,000 per student per year for campus study and $5,000 per student for a year's training in the complex. The total cost of the annual output of 384,000 teachers would be about $4,224,000,000, or almost five times the estimated current expenditures for teacher education.

A Budget for Action

The initial outlay of money would be a fraction of the annual expenditure of about four billion dollars required to operate the program when it is fully developed. The program cannot begin full blown; it must be built step by step. The initial funding should be for the establishment of six training complexes to produce instructional materials. These complexes would not operate as training centers during the first two years, except for trying out materials. The first expenditures would therefore be for housing the complexes and supplying them with equipment and for the salary of production teams for a period of two years. We estimate that there would be one team of five members in the areas of theoretical knowledge, self-evaluation and self-control, subject matter analysis, and professional governance, and two teams in the area of training, one for the elementary and one for the secondary school. We estimate the cost of six complexes for a period of two years at $9,180,000, the cost of a single complex being arrived at as follows: establishing the training complex, $250,000; thirty staff members for two years at $18,000 each year, $1,080,000; and overhead, $200,000, or a total of $1,530,000.

The second phase is the training program for instructors who are to use the materials in the complexes and in theoretical courses in the colleges and universities. This phase should begin in the summer of the second year after materials have been prepared and tried out.

Training in the use of the materials can be carried on in summer workshops held at the training complexes. Each complex can accommodate ninety participants with a staff of about fifteen instructors representing each production team. The budget for the workshop staff would be approximately $72,000, assuming a salary of $4,000 per staff member and $12,000 for operating expenses. The total budget for six workshops, one at each complex, would be $432,000. In addition, a summer salary should be provided for each participant since most, if not all, participants would normally be employed as summer school instructors. The salary of the participants, however, should be paid by their respective institutions or public school systems.

The total cost of the first two years of the program (including the establishment of six complexes, production of training materials, and the preparation of 540 teacher trainers) would be a little more than nine and a half million dollars. With 540 staff members prepared to operate training complexes, eighteen new complexes can be established in the third year. Beginning with the fourth year, training complexes can be established at a very rapid rate, for twenty-four training centers could prepare 2,160 instructors in the summer of the third year. Seventy-two new centers could then be opened up. In the fifth year 288 new centers could be opened. This would probably be too fast a pace, because there would doubtless be operational and institutional problems to work out, and a slower pace would safeguard the program against overextension in the face of accumulating problems.

Where is the money coming from? Teacher education is a national task. It can no longer be considered a state function, dependent entirely upon local initiative and state support. To be sure, the higher institutions and training complexes must be partly financed by state and local funds, but the amount of funding required exceeds the available state and local revenue. It is therefore necessary for the federal government partly to underwrite the training complexes either through allocation of funds to state departments of education or directly to the complexes.

The support of training complexes by the federal government would represent a change in federal policy. It would mean the support of the basic program of teacher education. In its appropriation of funds for teacher training, the federal government has concentrated upon programs for experienced teachers and teacher aides. It has ignored the basic program of teacher education given by the colleges and universities, and, in fact, it has bypassed this program by setting up the teacher corps and other alternatives.

This policy of the federal government can be attributed to the failure of the teaching profession, and especially the group responsible for teacher preparation, to develop a comprehensive plan of teacher education for the nation. In the absence of planning for the education of its personnel by the profession, governmental agencies are likely to ride off in all directions. When no legitimate leadership is provided, all sorts of ill-conceived schemes will be put forward with enthusiasm, and adopted. The appropriate alternative is planning, and persistent advocacy of a program by the profession itself.

Teacher Education as a National Problem

In the preceding chapters we outlined a comprehensive approach to the development of a teacher education program from the level of teacher aide to that of the intern. This program covers an extensive span of time, a period in which the basic concepts, attitudes, and skills of the teacher can be shaped. It is therefore a crucial phase of a teacher's preparation. Work beyond the bachelor's degree has been dealt with briefly, and discussed primarily with the view to preparing the teacher for the increasing differentiation of roles and the burdens which community poverty and school integration place on him. There is need for a thorough treatment of graduate professional education of the teacher. But this essay must end at some point, and we chose to stop short of advanced professional work.

We have insisted again and again that any teacher who is adequately prepared is trained to cope with the problems and difficulties of pupils regardless of their social backgrounds or racial origins. The ability to teach the disadvantaged, like the ability to teach pupils who come from more advantaged strata of society, is viewed as one aspect of a teacher's total preparation. He is to be trained as a general practitioner and is not to be thought of as performing successfully only with certain social classes or ethnic groups.

We have also insisted that the preparation of the teacher suffers from inadequate programs. Teacher education is dominated by curriculums developed at the beginning of the present century when the graduate study of education was initiated and when very little was known about teaching and learning. Unfortunately, many of the current plans to improve teacher education tend to ignore the knowledge about learning and teaching accumulated in the last fifty years. As a result, they repeat many of the errors of the programs they are designed to replace. If teacher education is to meet the demand for teachers of professional quality, capable of meeting the challenge of an open society in these times, it must be based upon what is known about teaching behavior and learning and about the techniques and procedures of teacher training itself. The task of building this knowledge into instructional materials, and training the teacher educator to use them, is at the heart of the problem of teacher education today. This task is enormous, and the burden of coping with it is increased by the fact that the personnel that must prepare the materials and train itself to use them must at the same time carry on a program to supply almost 200,000 new teachers per year. Reforming teacher education is like rebuilding the wheels of a car in motion.

To educate teachers to operate in the complex society of today requires programs addressed to national needs. The pool of available manpower is not uniformly distributed throughout the country nor are training institutions of high quality equally distributed within the population. Furthermore, teacher training needs have long cut across state and local lines. It makes no better sense to recruit and train ghetto-born teachers exclusively for ghetto pupils than to train suburban-born teachers to teach suburban pupils. It is hardly logical to recruit New Yorkers to teach in and meet exclusively the needs of New York State, given the sprawl of greater New York into Connecticut and New Jersey, or the migration of New Yorkers into Florida, California, and Puerto Rico. A national thrust that sees beyond state and local lines is sorely needed. This does not mean divorce of operational recruiting and training mechanisms from state and local vehicles. It simply means utilizing and supporting such vehicles within the context of the national perspective on the recruitment and training of educational manpower.

Universities, both private and public, will be able to serve society more effectively if they can take the long-range, national view. Should New York City's educational training problems be the exclusive concern of New York City or New York universities? Is the problem of training teachers of the disadvantaged one which should preoccupy only those higher educational institutions located in disadvantaged areas? Programs with national thrust and responsibilities are needed to move universities, regardless of their source of support and location, to accept teacher education as a common national problem.

It is unrealistic to assume that local and state institutions and agencies can or should bear the major brunt for long-range planning and development of training programs to meet national needs. Particularly at a time when comprehensive and systematic approaches to teacher training are so desperately needed, there is a strong case for the federal government to assume part of the burden of long-range planning in cooperation with state and local institutions. Given the objective of an open society, it is essential that national revenues be made available for the initiation and continued support of such national teacher education projects as manpower recruitment, training programs, and materials development.

NOTES

Introduction

1. Hentoff, Nat. *Our Children Are Dying.* (Introduction by John Holt.) New York: Viking Press, 1966. 141 pp.
   See also
   Kozol, Jonathan. *Death at an Early Age.* Boston: Houghton Mifflin Co., 1967. 240 pp.
2. Emerson, Ralph Waldo. Address to Phi Beta Kappa, Cambridge, Massachusetts, August 31, 1837.
3. Van Doren, Mark, editor. *The Portable Emerson.* New York: Viking Press, 1965. pp. 4-5.

Chapter 1

1. Fantini, Mario D., and Weinstein, Gerald. *The Disadvantaged: Challenge to Education.* New York: Harper & Row, 1968. p. 382.
2. Frank, Virginia. *New Curricular Materials and the Teaching of the Disadvantaged* (Project Report/One). Washington, D.C.: The NDEA National Institute for Advanced Study in Teaching Disadvantaged Youth, July 1968. pp. 33-50.
3. Gerrard, Nathan L. *Disadvantaged Youth* (Occasional Paper/Three). Washington, D.C.: The NDEA National Institute for Advanced Study in Teaching Disadvantaged Youth, May 1968. pp. 13-24.
4. Little, Malcolm. *Malcolm X Speaks: Selected Speeches and Statements.* (Edited, with prefatory notes, by George Breitman.) New York: Merit Publishers, 1965. 242 pp.

Chapter 2

1. National Education Association, Research Division. *Teacher Supply and Demand in Public Schools, 1967.* Research Report 1967-R18. Washington, D.C.: the Association, 1967.
2. *Ibid.*
3. *Ibid.*
4. U. S. Department of Health, Education, and Welfare, Office of Education.

Education in the Seventies. Planning Paper 68-1. Washington, D.C.: Government Printing Office, 1968.

5. U. S. Bureau of the Census. *Census of Population, 1960. Detailed Characteristics.* United States Summary Final Report. P.C. (1)—ID. pp. 1-544, 1-547. Washington, D.C.: Government Printing Office, 1963.

6. Cohen, Elizabeth G. "Status of Teachers." *Review of Educational Research* 37: 280-95; June 1967.

7. Lieberman, Myron. *Education as a Profession.* Englewood Cliffs, N.J.: Prentice-Hall, 1956. 540 pp.

8. Strom, Robert D. *The Preface Plan: A New Concept of In-service Training for Teachers Newly Assigned to Urban Neighborhoods of Low Income.* Final Report, U. S. Department of Health, Education, and Welfare, Office of Education, Bureau of Research, Project No. 6-1365. Columbus, Ohio: The Ohio State University, 1967.

9. Strom, Robert D. *Ibid.*

10. Rossi, Peter H., and others. "Between White and Black: The Faces of American Institutions in the Ghetto." *Supplemental Studies to the National Advisory Commission on Civil Disorders.* Washington, D.C.: Government Printing Office, 1968. 248 pp.

11. Haubrich, Vernon F. "Teachers for Big-City Schools." *Education in Depressed Areas.* (Edited by A. Harry Passow.) New York: Teachers College, Columbia University, 1963. pp. 243-61.

12. Childs, John Lawrence. *Education and the Philosophy of Experimentalism.* New York: Century Co., 1931. 264 pp.

Chapter 3

1. Bowman, Garda W., and Klopf, Gordon J. *New Careers and Roles in the American School.* New York: Bank Street College of Education, 1967. pp. 3-6.
    See also
    Pearl, Arthur, and Riessman, Frank. *New Careers for the Poor: The Nonprofessional in Human Services.* New York: Free Press, 1965. 273 pp.; and
    Riessman, Frank. "Instant New Careers." *New Careers Newsletter* 2: 1-2; Spring 1968. (New York: New York University, New Careers Development Center.)

2. "New Horizons in Staff Utilization." *The Bulletin* 42: 1-213; January 1958. (Washington, D.C.: National Association of Secondary-School Principals.)

3. "New Careers Movement." *New Careers Newsletter* 1: 3; April 30, 1967. (New York: New York University, New Careers Development Center.)

4. Trump, J. Lloyd, and Baynham, Dorsey. *Guide to Better Schools.* Chicago: Rand McNally & Co., 1961. p. 139.
    See also
    National Commission on Teacher Education and Professional Standards, National Education Association. *Auxiliary School Personnel.* Washington, D.C.: the Association, 1967. 20 pp.

Chapter 4

1. Broudy, Harry S., Smith, B. Othanel, and Burnett, Joe R. *Democracy and Excellence in American Secondary Education.* Chicago: Rand McNally & Co., 1964. 302 pp.

2. Kozol, Jonathan. *Death at an Early Age.* Boston: Houghton Mifflin Co., 1967. 240 pp.

Chapter 5

1. Gage, Nathaniel L., editor. *Handbook of Research on Teaching.* Chicago: Rand McNally & Co., 1963. 1218 pp.
2. Schueler, Herbert, and Lesser, Gerald S. *Teacher Education and the New Media.* Washington, D.C.: American Association of Colleges for Teacher Education, 1967. pp. 21-24.
3. Flanders, Ned A. *Teacher Influence, Pupil Attitudes, and Achievement.* U.S. Office of Education Cooperative Research Project No. 397. Minneapolis: University of Minnesota, 1960. 121 pp.
   See also
   Flanders, Ned A. "Teacher Influence in the Classroom." *Theory and Research in Teaching.* (Edited by Arno A. Bellack.) New York: Teachers College, Columbia University, 1963. Chapter 4, pp. 37-52.
4. Bellack, Arno A., and others. *The Language of the Classroom.* New York: Teachers College Press, 1967. 274 pp.
5. Medley, Donald M., and Mitzel, Harold E. "Measuring Classroom Behavior by Systematic Observation." *Handbook of Research on Teaching.* (Edited by Nathaniel L. Gage.) Chicago: Rand McNally & Co., 1963. Chapter 6, pp. 247-328.
6. Flanders, Ned A., *op. cit.*
7. Smith, B. Othanel. "Recent Research on Teaching." *The High School Journal* 51: 63-74; November 1967.
8. Biddle, Bruce J., and Adams, Raymond S. *An Analysis of Classroom Activities.* U.S. Office of Education Contract No. 3-20-002. Columbia: University of Missouri, 1967.
9. Smith, B. Othanel, and others. *A Study of the Strategies of Teaching.* U.S. Office of Education Cooperative Research Project No. 1640. Urbana: University of Illinois, 1967.
10. Bellack, Arno A., and others, *op. cit.*
11. Smith, B. Othanel, and others, *op. cit.*
12. Spaulding, Robert L. *Achievement, Creativity, and Self-Concept Correlates of Teacher-Pupil Transactions in Elementary Schools.* U.S. Office of Education Cooperative Research Project No. 1352. Urbana: University of Illinois, 1963.
13. *Ibid.*
14. Kooi, Beverly, and Schutz, Richard. "A Factor Analysis of Classroom-Disturbance Intercorrelations." *American Educational Research Journal* 2: 37-40; January 1965.

Chapter 6

1. Pearl, Arthur, and Belton, Sylvia. *Final Report of the Bethel Project.* Washington, D.C.: NDEA National Institute for Advanced Study in Teaching Disadvantaged Youth, November 1967. 8 pp.
2. McDonald, Frederick J., and Allen, Dwight W. *Training Effects of Feedback and Modeling Procedures on Teaching Performance.* Palo Alto, California: Stanford University, 1967. p. 191.
3. Turner, Richard L. *Problem Solving Proficiency Among Elementary School Teachers II. Teachers of Arithmetic, Grades 3-6.* U.S. Office of Education Cooperative Research Project No. 419. Bloomington: Indiana University, 1960. p. 11.
4. Wade, Eugene W. *Problem Solving Proficiency Among Elementary School Teachers III. Teachers of Reading, Grades 2-5.* Monograph of the Institute of Educational Research, School of Education, Indiana University. Bloomington: Indiana University, 1961. p. 4.

5. McDonald, Frederick L., and Allen, Dwight W., *op. cit.*, p. 2.
6. *Ibid.*, pp. 3-4.
7. *Ibid.*, p. 153.
8. *Ibid.*, pp. 158-61.

Chapter 7

1. Peck, Robert F., and Bown, Oliver H. "Introduction." *The Research and Development Center for Teacher Education.* Austin: University of Texas, 1968. *Passim.* (Mimeo.)
2. Peck, Robert F. "Student Mental Health. The Range of Personality Patterns in a College Population." *Personality Factors on the College Campus.* (Edited by Robert F. Peck.) Austin: University of Texas, Hogg Foundation for Mental Health, 1962. pp. 161-99; 166-67.
3. Peck, Robert F., and Bown, Oliver H., *op. cit.*, pp. 3-4.
4. Fuller, Frances F., Bown, Oliver H., and Peck, Robert F. *Creating Climate for Growth.* Austin: University of Texas, Hogg Foundation for Mental Health, 1967. p. 21.
5. *Ibid.*, p. 17.
6. Fuller, Frances F., and others. *Effects of Personalized Feedback During Teacher Preparation on Teacher Personality and Teaching Behavior.* Austin: University of Texas, 1968. pp. 157-58. (Mimeo.)
7. *Ibid.*, pp. 158-60.
8. Myrdal, Gunnar, and others. *An American Dilemma.* New York: Harper & Brothers, 1944. Appendices 1, 2, and 3.
9. Berelson, Bernard, and Steiner, Gary A. *Human Behavior: An Inventory of Scientific Findings.* New York: Harcourt, Brace & World, 1964. pp. 537-38.
10. *Ibid.*, pp. 539-40.

Chapter 8

1. Smith, E. Brooks, and others, editors. *Partnership in Teacher Education.* Washington, D. C.: American Association of Colleges for Teacher Education, 1968. 296 pages.
   See also
   Sausalito Teacher Education Project. *Final Report.* San Francisco: San Francisco State College, Sausalito Teacher Education Project Clearing House, 1966. 119 pp.
2. Rice, Joseph Mayer. *The Public-School System of the United States.* New York, 1893.
3. Myrdal, Gunnar, and others. *An American Dilemma.* New York: Harper & Brothers, 1944. Appendices 1, 2, and 3.
4. *Ibid.*

Chapter 9

1. Smith, B. Othanel. "Knowledge About Knowledge for Teachers." *The Nature of Knowledge: Implications for the Education of Teachers.* (Edited by William A. Jenkins.) Milwaukee: University of Wisconsin, 1961.
2. Foshay, Arthur W. "Knowledge and the Structure of the Disciplines." *The Nature of Knowledge: Implications for the Education of Teachers.* (Edited by William A. Jenkins.) Milwaukee: University of Wisconsin, 1961.
3. *Ibid.*
4. Hocking, William E. "Dutch Higher Education: Comparative Impressions of a Visiting Harvard Professor." *Harvard Education Review* 20: 28-35; January 1950.

5. Bell, Daniel. *Reforming General Education.* New York: Columbia University Press, 1966. 320 pp.
6. Dewey, John. *Logic, The Theory of Inquiry.* New York: Henry Holt and Company, 1938. 546 pp.
7. National Advisory Commission on Civil Disorders. "Racial Attitudes of Urban Teachers." Supplemental Studies to the National Advisory Commission on Civil Disorders. Washington, D.C.: Government Printing Office, 1968. 248 pp.
8. Frank, Virginia. *New Curricular Materials and the Teaching of the Disadvantaged.* (Project Report/One) Washington, D.C.: NDEA National Institute for Advanced Study in Teaching Disadvantaged Youth, 1968. 64 pp.

Chapter 10

1. Smith, B. Othanel. Unpublished study.
2. Henderson, Kenneth B. "Uses of 'Subject Matter'." *Language and Concepts in Education.* (Edited by B. Othanel Smith and Robert H. Ennis.) Chicago: Rand McNally & Co., 1961. Chapter 3, pp. 43-58.
   See also
   Smith, B. Othanel. "Knowledge About Knowledge for Teachers." *The Nature of Knowledge: Implications for the Education of Teachers.* (Edited by William A. Jenkins.) Milwaukee: University of Wisconsin, 1961.
3. Smith, B. Othanel, and others. *A Study of the Logic of Teaching.* Urbana, Illinois: Bureau of Educational Research, 1962.
4. Fantini, Mario D., and Weinstein, Gerald. *The Disadvantaged: Challenge to Education.* New York: Harper & Row, 1968. pp. 337-73.
5. Broudy, Harry S., and others. *Democracy and Excellence in American Secondary Education.* Chicago: Rand McNally & Co., 1964. pp. 43-74.
6. Deane, Paul C. "The Persistence of Uncle Tom: An Examination of the Image of the Negro in Children's Fiction Series." *Journal of Negro Education* 37: 140-45; Spring 1968.
7. Waite, Richard R. "Further Attempts to Integrate and Urbanize First Grade Reading Textbooks. A Research Study." *Journal of Negro Education* 37; Winter 1968.

Chapter 11

1. Lindsey, Margaret, editor. *New Horizons for the Teaching Profession.* Washington, D.C.: National Commission on Teacher Education and Professional Standards of the National Education Association, 1961. p. 24.
2. Unpublished survey made of selected sample of National Education Association members, 1966.
3. National Commission on Teacher Education and Professional Standards of the National Education Association. *Guidelines for Professional Standards Boards.* Washington, D.C.: the Commission, January 1967. 14 pp. (Offset)
4. Mayor, John R., and Swartz, Willis G. *Accreditation in Teacher Education, Its Influence on Higher Education.* Washington, D.C.: National Commission on Accrediting, 1965. 311 pp.

Chapter 12

1. Klopf, Gordon J., and Bowman, Garda W. *Teacher Education in a Social Context.* New York: Mental Health Materials Center, 1966. pp. 238-58.
2. National Commission on Teacher Education and Professional Standards of the National Education Association. *Remaking the World of the Career Teacher.* Report of the 1965-66 Regional TEPS Conference. Washington, D.C.: the Association, 1966. *Passim.*

180

3. Strom, Robert D. The Preface Plan: *A New Concept of In-service Training for Teachers Newly Assigned to Urban Neighborhoods of Low Income.* Columbus: Ohio State University, August 1967. *Passim.*
   See also
   Tanner, James R. "In-service Training for Teachers of the Disadvantaged." *Education and the Disadvantaged.* (Edited by Harvey Goldman.) Milwaukee: University of Wisconsin-Milwaukee, School of Education, August 1967. pp. 53-64.
4. American Association of Colleges for Teacher Education. *Teacher Education: Issues and Innovations.* Twenty-first Yearbook. Washington, D.C.: the Association, 1968. 364 pp.

PUBLICATIONS

NDEA National Institute for Advanced Study in Teaching Disadvantaged Youth: 1967-1968

The Atlanta Area Workshop on Preparing Teachers to Work with Disadvantaged Youth. (Report/Two). 24 pp.

The Bethel Project. Sylvia Belton and Arthur Pearl, University of Oregon. (Project Report/Three). 8 pp.

Design and Default in Teacher Education. Vernon Haubrich, University of Wisconsin. (Occasional Paper/Two). 8 pp.

A Field Experience Guide. Calvin Eland, Red River Valley IIPD Project. (Materials/One). 8 pp.

The Identification and Analysis of Perceived Problems of Teachers in Inner-City Schools. Donald Cruickshank and James Leonard, University of Tennessee. (Occasional Paper/One). 12 pp.

New Curricular Materials and the Teaching of the Disadvantaged. Virginia Frank. (Project Report/One). 64 pp.

Obstacles to Change: The Westchester Report. Vernon Haubrich, University of Wisconsin. (Occasional Paper/Four). 4 pp.

Perceived Problems of Rural Classroom Teachers of the Disadvantaged. Donald Cruickshank and others, University of Tennessee. (Occasional Paper/Five). 16 pp.

The Preparation of Urban Teachers: A Syllabus. Harry N. Rivlin and Valda Robinson, Fordham University. (Working Papers/One). 220 pp.

Studies in Deprivation. Vernon Haubrich (ed.). (Occasional Paper/Special). 64 pp.

The Subject of Issues: Defining Central Problems and Questions in Preparing Teachers of Disadvantaged Youth. Helen J. Kenney, Clark University. (Report/Four). 16 pp.

Teacher Education: The Young Teacher's View. William C. Kvaraceus, Helen J. Kenney and Polly Bartholomew. (Project Report/Two). 48 pp.

Temple University Seminar: Language Education for the Disadvantaged. Russell A. Hill and Norma F. Furst, Temple University. (Report/Three). 32 pp.

Three Conferences: Urbanization, Work and Education; Youth in a Changing Society; Teacher Education in a New Context. (Project Report/Four). 40 pp.

Two Papers from the Appalachia Cooperative Program in Teacher Education. O. Norman Simpkins, Marshall University, and Nathan L. Gerard, Morris Harvey College. (Occasional Paper/Three). 24 pp.

The Yale Conference on Learning. Edward F. Zigler and Willa Abelson, Yale University. (Report/One). 8 pp.

American Association of Colleges for Teacher Education

Changing Dimensions in Teacher Education. Proceedings of the Nineteenth Annual Meeting. 1967. 300 pp.

Conceptual Models in Teacher Education: An Approach to Teaching and Learning. John R. Verduin, Jr. 1967. 140 pp.

Partnership in Teacher Education. Edited by E. Brooks Smith, Hans C. Olsen, Patrick J. Johnson, and Chandler Barbour. 1968. 308 pp.

Professional Teacher Education: A Programed Design Developed by the AACTE Teacher Education and Media Project. 1968. 84 pp.

Professional Teacher Education II: A Programed Design Developed by the AACTE Teacher Education and Media Project. A Report on Workshops in Teacher Education. 1969. 94 pp.

Teacher Education: Issues and Innovations. Proceedings of the Twentieth Annual Meeting. 1968. 374 pp.

Teacher Education and the New Media. Herbert Schueler and Gerald S. Lesser. 1967. 130 pp.

The World and the American Teacher: The Preparation of Teachers in the Field of World Affairs. Harold Taylor. 1968. 320 pp.

All publications on pages 181 and 182 may be ordered from the American Association of Colleges for Teacher Education, 1201 Sixteenth Street, N.W., Washington, D.C. 20036. A complete publications list is available on request.

American Association of University
Professors, 170,
and quality of teacher education,
170-171
Attitudes: teacher, 61
other-oriented, 90
teacher, modification of, 91-92

Bank Street College of Education, 154,
study of NDEA Institutes, 154-155
Barzun, Jacques: quoted, 117
Bellack, Arno, 54-56
Bethel project, 68
Bias in subject matter, 6, 133-134
Bureaucracy: effects of, 1-2

Canadian Federation of Teachers, 144
Coleman Report, 15, 22
Community: role of, in training complex, 96-98
as source of clients, 101
Concepts: as theoretical knowledge, 42
uses of, 44-46, 131-133
relation to teacher attitudes, 45
role in teacher education, 46ff.
in teaching, 56
and modes of input, 57-59
as basis of general education, 116,
118
as form of subject matter, 127-128
Content of instruction: preparation of
teachers in, 119-122

Cost of training teachers, 170-172
Courses: systematic, in theory, 64
in teacher education, 48-49, 156
Cumulation: principle of, 107-109

Democritus, 116
Desegregation: and the power structure, 18-19
preparing teachers for, 159-161
Dewey, John, 116
Disadvantaged: false ideas about,
13-14
and deprivation, 14-16
and discrimination by the schools,
15-16
and racism, 16-18
preparation of teachers for, 157-159,
passim
Disciplines: relation to professional
study, 42-44
definition of, 113-114
teacher preparation in, 114-115
criticism of discipline-oriented programs, 116-119

Education Professions Development
Act, 33, 141
Educational service districts, 104-105
Educational technology, 52-53
Elementary and Secondary Education
Act, 33

Factual knowledge, 43
  as form of subject matter, 128-129
Federal support of teacher education, 173
Feedback, 78-79
  absence of, in student teaching, 70
  primary, 78
  secondary, 78
  immediate vs. delayed, 79
  in relation to self attitudes in teaching, 86ff.
Field: definition of, 113-114
Flanders, N. A., 54-55
Forms of subject matter: knowledge about, 127-129

Gage, N. L., 54
Governance of the profession: teacher preparation in, 135-149

Haubrich, Vernon, 26,
  quoted, 28
Hendrix College, 104
Hocking, William E., 116

Indiana University, 104
Institutes: NDEA, evaluation of, 154-155
Instructional labor: division of, 31-32
Integration of the schools, 18-19
Intern: definition of, 102
  program, 102-103

Kerner Report, 15
Knowledge: theoretical, as basis of teaching, 42-43
  factual, 43
  practical, 43
  theoretical, in interpretation, 44-45
  theoretical, in problem solving, 45-46
  replicative use of, 46
  theoretical, in teacher education, 46-49
  associative use of, 131-132
  interpretive use of, 132
  applicative use of, 132
  about subject matter, 125-134
  forms of, 127-129

Malcolm X: control of the schools, 18-19
Marx, Karl, 106
MAT-type programs: criticism of, 70, 102
Mayor study, 143
Myrdal, Gunnar, 107

National Advisory Commission on Civil Disorders, 28, 121
National Council for the Accreditation of Teacher Education, 143, 148
National Defense Education Act, 154
National Science Foundation, 120
National Teacher Corps, 68, 69, 155, 173

Objectives of education: in a free society, 3,
  in relation to disadvantaged, 3-7
Observation systems for teaching behavior, 54-56

Peck, Robert, 82, 83
Perennial teacher education: purposes of, 151-153
  critique of existing programs, 153-156
  teachers for, 161-163
Personality: definition of, 81-82
  role in teaching, 81-83
  and self-management, 83-89
  need for a program of self-study, 92ff.
Program Development: procedures of, 64-65, 77
Protocol materials, 52-53
  use of, in teacher education, 62-64
  and training teachers of the disadvantaged, 158
Provincialism, among teachers, 139

Racial Isolation Report, 15
Racism: in teacher education, 2-3
Relevance of subject matter: teacher preparation in knowledge about, 130-133
Rice, Joseph M., 106

Schools: integration of, 18-19
Segregation: effects of, 2
Subject matter: definition of, 111-112
  preparation of teachers in, 112-113
  preparation of teachers, cooperative planning in, 122-123
  ways of talking about, 126
  forms of, 127-129
  logical aspects of, 129-130
  relevance of, 130-133
  bias in, 133-134
Subject of instruction: definition of, 114
Sumner, William G., 106

Strategies: in funding, 10
in teacher education, 105-109
student teaching, 70, 102

Teacher aides, 33
number of, 34
activities of, 35
training of, 36-37
recruitment of, 37-39
in training complex, 96
Teacher attitudes, 61
other-oriented, 90
modification of, 91-92
Teacher education: reform in, 8-10
as related to deprivation and racism,
11-20
and dialect, 5-6, 11
for the culturally deprived, 12-13,
passim
and school integration, 19-20, 159-
161
role of philosophy in, 49, 62, 64, 156
and conceptual system, 51-65
and protocol materials, 52-53, 62-64
and interpretation of teaching situations, 57-58
and identifying and analyzing pupil
errors, 58-59
and interpreting interpersonal relationships, 59-60
and conduct situations, 60-61
and extraclassroom situations, 62
and psychological concepts, 62-63
current programs of, 67-70
abilities to be developed in a program of, 71
affective aspects of, 81-93
and attitudes, 90
program for affective aspects of,
92-93
in the disciplines, 114-115
as perennial, 151-163
as perennial, critique of existing programs, 153-156
as a national problem, 166-167
plan of action for a program of,
167-169
program, budget for, 172-173
federal support of, 173
Teachers: supply of, 21-22
desirable attributes of, 7-8
causes of exodus from the profession, 22-26
attrition in deprived areas, 26-29
in deprived areas, deficiencies in
training of, 28-29
differentiated roles of, 31-32

situations faced by, 52
subject matter preparation of, 111-
123
preparation in content of instruction,
119-122
provincialism among, 139
retirement of, 140
cost of adequate training of, 171-172
cost of present training of, 170-171
Teaching: theoretical basis of, 42-44
complexity of, 69
role of personality in, 81-83
profession, a concept of, 136-140
profession as an entity: a design
for, 141-149
Technology: educational, 52-53
Theoretical knowledge, 42-43
and interpretation, 44-45, 56-64
in problem solving, 45-46
in teacher education, 46-49
in diagnosing pupil errors, 58-59
Training: concept of, 70-71
situations, 72-78
materials for, 77-78
in self-management, 83-89
of teachers in logic of subject matter, 129-130
of teachers in knowledge about
relevance of subject matter,
130-133
of teachers in the governance of the
profession, 135-149
program for teachers, cost of, 170-
172
complex, estimated cost of, 172
Training complex, 95-109
functions of, 95-96
role of community in, 96-98
organization of, 98-99
staff of, 99-100
source of pupils and clients, 101-102
number of, 103-105
optimum number of trainees per, 104
criticisms of, 105-109
producing materials for, 167-168
testing materials for, 168-169
Triple-T Project, 161
Tutors: pupil, 33

Unity: substantive, as basis of general
education, 116-119
Universal method: doctrine of, 116-117
as basis of general education, 117-
118

Vocational Education Act: 1968
amendments to, 33